The Bible On
The Final Coming

The Bible

on

The Final

Coming

by H. DE BAAR C.M.

Translated by F. Vander Heijden, O. Praem.

ST. NORBERT ABBEY PRESS
De Pere, Wisconsin
U. S. A.
1965

Biblical quotations are from the Revised Standard Version of the Bible, copyrighted 1946 and 1952 by the Division of Christian Education, National Council of Churches, and used by permission.

Nihil obstat:

> Samuel D. Jadin, O. Praem.
> Censor deputatus

Imprimatur:

> †Stanislaus V. Bona, D.D.
> Bishop of Green Bay
> November 30, 1965

> The *Nihil obstat* and *Imprimatur* are a declaration that a book or pamphlet is considered free from doctrinal or moral error. It is not implied that those who have granted the *Nihil obstat* and *Imprimatur* agree with the contents, opinions or statements expressed.

Originally published as
De Bijbel over de wederkomst van Christus
Roermond and Maaseik, J. J. Romen & Zonen, 1961

Library of Congress catalogue card number: 65 - 29092

Printed in the United States of America
ST. NORBERT ABBEY PRESS
De Pere, Wisconsin

CONTENTS

FOREWORD

In the seventh article of our Creed we pray: "From thence he shall come to judge the living and the dead." Christ, who ascended into heaven will return to judge the world.

In this book we hope to develop this truth with some light from the Bible. One who reads the New Testament will notice how often the return of Christ is mentioned. This proves its importance.

But, one must remember too that this is a very complicated theme and must not suppose that he will find, everywhere, identical statements about this return. The New Testament shows many traces of a development of the expectation for this return.

We should remember that nearly all the authors of the New Testament are of semitic origin and they have not belied this origin. Therefore we must distinguish between the truth which they wish to teach and their own peculiar way of expression. We must separate the essential from the accidental. The purpose of this book is to draw this to the attention of the reader.

THE EXPECTATION OF
GOD'S COMING

What the Bible, especially the New Testament, says about the return of Christ is a part of eschatology, i.e. the doctrine about the last things, **the eschata.**

To form an idea what the New Testament teaches about the return of Christ, it is absolutely necessary to consider the eschatology of the Old Testament and of the Jews. This must be done not only because Christ always mentions them, but also because his coming is the fulfillment of the Old Testament expectation of God's coming to bring salvation. We find this expectation mentioned in many places. Several psalms describe the coming of God to judge the world and to reign as king. This expectation has not always been the same; we must try to trace its development.

Israel expected God's salvation because it had experienced the mighty deeds of Yahweh, its God. The expectation is as old as Yahwism. From such historical experiences as its liberation from Egypt, Israel gained the conviction that Yahweh was mighty,

that he directed all events and led them according
to his own wishes. The fact that he had directed
these events in the past was for Israel a guarantee
that he would do the same in the future. Yahweh
achieves whatever he wants. Israel knew that Yahweh
is a God who brings salvation. On its experiences
it built its expectation for the future. Yahweh had
designed something great for Israel. Just exactly
what his design was, they were to learn only grad-
ually. In the beginning they thought that this wonderful future would consist in earthly welfare, a
fertile country, fertility of men and cattle and victory
over their enemies. Very early, shortly after their
settlement in Canaan, they developed the idea that
a king would be the ideal person to realize these
expectations. The king is "the Lord's anointed" (1
Sam. 26, 9); he represents Yahweh and symbolizes
the welfare of the people. During the time of the
kings there arose in Israel the expectation of a
Messiah (Anointed One), who would bring about
God's salvation. This expectation has its origin in
the prophecy of Nathan to David, which connects
the messianic expectation with David: "Your house
and your kingdom shall be made sure for ever before
me; your throne shall be established for ever" (2
Sam. 7, 16). Henceforth the expectation of God's
favor in Israel is seen coming to them through the
dynasty of David.

The knowledge that Israel was as yet surrounded
by enemies and the conviction that they were God's
chosen people were causes of their awaiting "a day

of Yahweh": an intervention of Yahweh to bring about a decision against their enemies and to bring about the complete salvation of Israel. This intervention of Yahweh was something that lay entirely on a national and political level. The prophet Amos however, the first of the so called writing prophets, gives a warning against such a hope: "Woe to you who desire the day of the Lord! Why should you have the day of the Lord? It is darkness, and not light" (5, 18). In metaphoric language he expresses the idea that this day will be a fatal day for Israel. For when Yahweh comes he will punish sins and crimes, and these have also been committed by Israel. Its election is exactly the reason why it deserves punishment. Sinners cannot expect blessing only calamity. Only a conversion of heart can protect a morally depraved Israel against the imminent punishment of the day of Yahweh. The other prophets before the exile speak in the same way: Hosea, Isaiah, Micah, Zephania, Jeremiah and Ezekiel. All of them are convinced that Israel deserves punishment and that it will not be able to escape this unless it is converted. Yet this expectation of God's salvation never vanished. Yahweh will bring salvation, but only to the small group of faithful which will be left after the judgment: "the rest of Israel." Evidently for the prophets the day of Yahweh has a moral character; it is the day of judgment, on which Yahweh will settle accounts with sin, his only enemy. On this day the just and the sinners will be separated; for the sinners it is a day of punishment, for the just a day of salvation. Because this day is looked

upon as judgment day, it is also called "a day
of wrath" (Zeph. 1, 15). It is not certain that this
day of Yahweh is considered by the prophets as a
day of definitive reckoning, or as a purification of
Israel. Moreover it is difficult to distinguish from
their words whether the day of judgment comprises
all peoples, though surely other peoples are concerned with it. In Zephania the judgment is universal
and comprises the whole world: "I will utterly sweep
away everything from the face of the earth, says the
Lord. I will sweep away man and beast; I will sweep
away the birds of the air and the fish of the sea.
I will overthrow the wicked; I will cut off mankind
from the face of the earth, says the Lord" (1, 2-3).

In those days the kings led the people into evil.
Therefore it was not these kings who would bring
about the salvation of Yahweh. The prophet Isaiah
does not consider the reigning kings as the bearers
of the messianic promises. He believes in the mission of the dynasty of David and he points toward a
descendant of David, who still must come, as the
one who will bring about this salvation. He stresses
the moral qualifications of this Messiah and shows
how God will work through him: "Behold, a young
woman shall conceive and bear a son, and shall
call his name Emmanuel. He shall eat curds and
honey when he knows how to refuse the evil and
choose the good" (7, 14-15). "For to us a child is
born, to us a son is given; and the government will
be upon his shoulder, and his name will be called
Wonderful Counselor, Mighty God, Everlasting Father, Prince of Peace! Of the increase of his govern-

ment and of peace there will be no end, upon the throne of David and over his kingdom, to establish it and uphold it with justice and righteousness from this time forth and for evermore. The zeal of the Lord of hosts will do this" (9, 5-6). The time in which this salvation of Yahweh will be realized will know no sin or evil: "They shall not hurt or destroy in all my holy mountain; for the earth shall be full of knowledge of the Lord as the waters cover the sea" (11, 9). Once more the world will be the same as it was in the days of paradise. The other prophets show similar expectations.

The attempts of the prophets to bring the people to conversion did not meet with lasting success. Punishment consequently is unavoidable. In 722 Samariah was taken; in 587 Jerusalem; and this meant a severe crisis for the expectation of Israel; but the faith of the prophets never wavered. Jeremiah and Ezekiel keep alive the expectation that Yahweh will intervene and that the misery of Israel will come to an end. The rest of Israel which is left will convert itself and Yahweh will enter into a new covenant with it: "But this is the covenant which I will make with the house of Israel after those days, says the Lord: I will put my law within them, and I will write it upon their hearts; and I will be their God, and they shall be my people" (Jer. 31, 33). The salvation which Yahweh will bring about will be chiefly a liberation from the slavery of sin; stress is placed upon interior renewal: "They shall not defile themselves any more with their idols . . . I

will save them from all the backslidings in which
they have sinned, and will cleanse them; and they
shall be my people, and I will be their God" (Ezek.
37, 23). Then Yahweh's blessings will also include
temporal welfare. Both prophets still expect this
salvation through a Messiah of the house of David,
who will reign over a reunited Israel, and who will
bring the people happiness and welfare; but the
chief stress lies on the moral character of God's
salvation: "Behold, the days are coming, says the
Lord, when I will raise up for David a righteous
Branch, and he shall reign as king and deal wisely,
and shall execute justice and righteousness in the
land" (Jer. 23, 5). "My servant David shall be king
over them; and they shall all have one shepherd.
They shall follow my ordinances and be careful to
observe my statutes. They shall dwell in the land
where your fathers dwelt that I gave to my servant
Jacob; they and their children and the children's
children shall dwell there for ever" (Ezech. 37, 24-25).

In these dark days we see that the prophets expect
not only that the "remnant" of a new Israel shall be
built up again, but also that Israel will be the
religious center of the whole world. "It shall come
to pass in the latter days that the mountains of the
house of the Lord shall be established as the highest
of the mountains and shall be raised above the hills;
and all the nations shall flow to it, and many people
shall come, and say: Come, let us go up to the
mountain of the Lord, to the house of the God of
Jacob; that he may teach us his ways and that we

may walk in the paths" (Is. 2, 2-5; Mik. 4, 1-3). These are the first signs that the salvation which Israel expected was no longer seen as something national, but as something universal, destined for all nations.

Toward the end of the exile, the so called second Isaiah (Is. 40-55) announces that Yahweh will intervene in order to restore Israel. Israel has done penance; Yahweh has mercy on it again and will lead it back to its country, as he led it out of Egypt. He will reign in Jerusalem: "How beautiful upon the mountains are the feet of him who brings good tidings, who publishes peace, who brings good tidings of good, who publishes salvation, who says to Zion: Your God reigns" (52, 7). This reign of God will be a reign of righteousness; the people will know the law and keep it in their hearts (51, 7); the days of paradise will return: "For the Lord will comfort Zion; he will comfort all her waste places, and will make her wilderness the Eden, her desert like the garden of the Lord; joy and gladness will be found in her, thanksgiving and the voice of song" (51, 3) and this will last without end.

Among the exiles who returned in 538 to their country were the prophets Haggai and Zechariah who point out to the people the salvation which is approaching. When the temple is being rebuilt Haggai prophesies: "The latter splendor of this house shall be greater than the former, says the Lord of hosts; and in this place I will give prosperity, says the Lord of hosts" (Hag. 2, 9). Other nations, too, will acknowledge Yahweh: "Many peoples and

strong nations shall come to seek the Lord of hosts
in Jerusalem, and to entreat the favor of the Lord"
(Zech. 8, 22). Both these prophets seem to expect
that their contemporary, Zerubbabel, grandson of
Jojakim, will be the Messiah: "On that day, says
the Lord of hosts, I will take you, O Zerubbabel my
servant, the son of She-alti-el, says the Lord, and
make you like a signet ring; for I have chosen you,
says the Lord of hosts" (Hag. 2, 23).

The songs of the Servant of Yahweh (Is. 42, 1-7;
49, 1-9; 50, 4-11; 52, 13-53; 12) announce the conversion of pagans through the sufferings of this Servant:
"He says: Is it too light a thing that you should
be my servant to raise up the tribes of Jacob and
to restore the preserved of Israel; I will give you
as a light to the nations, that my salvation may
reach to the end of the earth" (Is. 49, 6). "By his
knowledge shall the righteous one, my servant, make
many to be accounted righteous; and he shall bear
their iniquities. Therefore I will divide him a
portion with the great, and he shall divide the spoil
with the strong" (Is. 53, 11-12). Christ will identify
himself with this Servant.

We see that the expectation of Israel has gone
through a development since the time of the exile:
it is no longer national and exterior, but universal
and interior.

This expectation, however, was not fulfilled. The
moral conversion of the people did not take place.
The dynasty of David was not restored; the Messiah

never came and the golden age never dawned. Again a crisis threatened: at this time the third Isaiah (56-66) announces that because of the sinfulness of the world the salvation which God would bring about would be something belonging to another world: "For behold, I create new heavens and a new earth; and the former things shall not be remembered or come into mind" (65, 17). In Malachi we see that many people resented the fact that the day of Yahweh and the final decision never came. "You have wearied the Lord with your words. Yet you say: How have we wearied him? By saying: Every one who does evil is good in the sight of the Lord, and he delights in them. Or by asking: Where is the God of justice?" (Mal. 2, 17). He assures them that the day of judgment will come. This is also stressed by Joel and the second Zechariah (9-14), who announce the day of Yahweh which will precede the new world: A day of wrath, but the just will be saved.

Beginning with the second century it is chiefly the apocalyptic writings which give us information about the expectation of the people. The word "apocalyptic" is derived from a Greek word which means "to reveal." It is a literary genre very much in vogue since the second century B. C., though initial traces of it are already found with the prophets, such as Joel, the second Zechariah, Ezekiel and the apocalypse (24-27). This apocalyptic vision wants to reveal the future, especially the last days. Preferably, they introduce a person of the past (e.g. Henoch) as speaking about visions of the future. This future is described in symbols and this expectation is intended to console the people in the difficult circumstances in which they live. The critical situation in which the Jews of those days found themselves explains the success of such writing. Most of these apocalypses belong to the apocrypha, i.e. the books which because of their title or their contents show some resemblance to Holy Scripture, but are not considered belonging to it. Such apocryphal books, nevertheless, may faithfully reflect authentic traditions of Israel, though there are also writings which indulge in fanciful descriptions. Because of this the expectation of the people became quite chaotic.

We find the most famous apocalypses of this time in the biblical book of Daniel. This was written during the persecutions of Antioch IV Epiphanes (167-164). It consoles the Jews who were persecuted because of their faith, by the expectation of God's salvation, which will surely follow his judgment of Antioch and the other enemies. The seventh chapter foretells that after the great political empires the reign of God will come. This reign is not an earthly but a heavenly one. "I saw in the night visions. And behold, with the clouds of heaven there came one like a Son of Man, and he came to the Ancient of Days and was presented before him. And to him was given dominion and glory and kingdom, that all peoples, nations and languages should serve him; his dominion is an everlasting dominion, which shall not pass away, and his kingdom one that shall not be destroyed" (7, 13-14). The explanation of this vision is given further on: "But . . . the kingdom and the dominion and the greatness of the kingdom under the whole heaven shall be given to the people of the saints of the Most High; their kingdom shall be an everlasting kingdom, and all dominions shall serve and obey them" (7, 27). This Son of Man represents the people of God and is at the same time the head of this people. The name does not indicate the Messiah of the house of David. Christ will identify himself with this Son of Man. This reign of God will be not only a reign over those who are living at that time, because its inception will be preceded by a resurrection: "And many of those who sleep in the dust of the earth shall awake, some to everlasting life, and some to shame and everlasting contempt. And those who are wise shall shine like the brightness of the firmament: and those who turn many to righteousness, like the stars for ever and ever" (12, 2-3). In this prophecy of the heavenly reign of God the prophecies of the Old Testament reach their zenith.

Daniel also describes the reign of God as if it does not belong to this time of history. He calls the time of persecution "the time of the end" (8, 17; 11, 35, 40) or "the end" (9, 26; 11, 27). The end of this time will be a time of distress (12, 1) and the judgment falls between this time and the new one.

The Jewish writings of this period continually speak about this theme of salvation. They distinguish between this age, the evil world. and the future age,

the new world of righteousness. They speak about
the Messiah and the usual traditional expectation of
the Son of David. Christ identifies himself with
these authentic traditions of the Jewish faith, but he
keeps aloof from chauvenistic and fantastic expectations rampant in his days, as we learn from the
gospel.

THE FULFILLMENT IN CHRIST

"In those days came John the Baptist preaching in the wilderness of Judea. Repent, for the kingdom of heaven is at hand" (Mt. 3, 1-2). John needs not give any further explanation: people understand that he means that the time has come to which the Old Testament has been looking forward.

Christ, too, as John did, announces that the kingdom of God has come: "Now after John was arrested, Jesus came to Galilee, preaching the gospel of God and saying: The time is fulfilled, and the kingdom of God is at hand; repent, and believe in the gospel" (Mk. 1, 14-15). "From the days of John the Baptist until now the kingdom of heaven has suffered violence, and men of violence take it by force. For all the prophets and the law prophesied until John" (Mt. 11, 12-13). "Then turning to the disciples he said privately: Blessed are the eyes which see what you see! For I tell you that many prophets and kings desired to see what you see, and did not see it, and to hear what you hear, and did not hear it" (Lk. 10, 23-24).

The New Testament not only testifies that at the time of Christ the expectations of the Old Testament were fulfilled, but it also tries to teach us that it is he himself in whom and through whom this fulfillment has come: Christ is the expected Messiah, the Son of Man, the suffering Servant of Yahweh.

The name "Christ" itself shows that he is the Messiah, because "Christ" is the Greek translation of the Hebrew word "Messiah" (Anointed One). The purpose of the gospel of Matthew is to prove that he is indeed the Messiah. John declares: "Now Jesus did many other signs in the presence of the disciples, which are not written in this book; but these are written that you may believe that Jesus is the Christ, the Son of God, and that believing you may have life in his name (Jn. 20, 30-31).

Christ avoids calling himself "Messiah." He does not want to be known as such (except during his entrance into Jerusalem). His reason seems to be his desire not to be identified with the false ideas about the coming Messiah which were prevalent among the people.

Before his resurrection Christ preferred to call himself "the Son of Man" and what strikes us is that nobody else gives him this title. He certainly had a purpose in using it. As a messianic title it was not in common use; moreover, Christ intended to show a connection between the Son of Man in Dan. 7, 13 and himself. He assumes for himself the heavenly character, the power and everything else that Daniel and the apocalyptic writers say about the Son of Man. By using this name he also points to the human and suffering character of this Son of Man, and in this way the connection with the suffering Servant is easily seen. Christ himself suggests that he is this suffering Servant: "For the Son of Man also came not to be served but to serve, and to give his life as a ransom for many" (Mk. 10, 45): Cf.: "Yet it was the will of the Lord to bruise him; he has put him to grief; when he makes himself (Hebr.: you make his soul) an offering for sin" (Is. 53, 10). In Luke we read that Christ says: "For I tell you that this scripture must be fulfilled in me: And he was reckoned with transgressors" (Lk. 22, 37; cf. Is. 53, 12).

Moreover, the evangelists consider his actions a fulfillment of the prophecies of the suffering Servant. When Matthew describes the healings which Christ performed he remarks that Christ did this "to fulfill what was spoken by the prophet Isaiah: He took our infirmities and bore our diseases" (Mt. 8, 17; cf. Is. 53, 4).

These are a few examples which show how the New Testament considers Christ fulfilling the expectation of salvation.

CHRIST THE JUDGE

Already in the texts which date from the last centuries B.C. we notice the idea that the real function of the Messiah will consist in being a judge.

In the New Testament we find the opinion clearly expressed that Christ is not only the Messiah, the Son of Man and the suffering Servant, but also that he is the one who will come to judge on the day of Yahweh.

The Baptist announces him in his penitential sermons as the future judge who will come: "His winnowing fork is in his hand, and he will clear his threshing floor and gather his wheat into the granary, but the chaff he will burn with unquenchable fire" (Mt. 3, 12; Lk. 3, 17). The Baptist expresses himself in a figurative language which is taken from the Old Testament prophets. The winnowing was a symbol of judgment and punishment (which were usually linked together in the prophets): "I have winnowed them with a winnowing fork in the gates of the land; I have bereaved them, I have destroyed my people; they did not turn from their ways" (Jer. 15, 7).

The disciples announce that Christ is the judge who will come at the end of time: "And he commanded us to preach to the people, and to testify that he is the one ordained by God to be judge of the living and the dead," Peter says to Cornelius (Acts 10, 42). Paul teaches the Corinthians: "For we must all appear before the judgment seat of Christ, so that each one may receive good or evil, according to what he has done in the body" (2 Cor. 5, 10).

Christ himself affirms that he is the judge of all men, living and dead. In the description of the last judgment it is evident that sentence is being passed by the Son of Man (Mt. 25, 31-46). In the Sermon on the Mount Christ, according to Matthew, says: "On that day many will say to me: Lord, Lord, did we not prophesy in your name, and cast out demons in your name, and do many mighty works in your name? And then will I declare to them: I never knew you; depart from me, you evildoers" (Mt. 7, 22-23). In the parable of the weeds among the wheat (Mt. 13, 24-30) he is the one who orders his servants to burn the weeds and to bring the wheat into his barns. "For the Son of Man is to come with his angels in the glory of his Father, and then he will repay every man for what he has done" (Mt. 16, 27).

There is no contradiction in the fact that, occasionally, in the New Testament it is said that God himself will judge; Paul does not contradict what he has said in 2 Cor. 5-10 when in another text he says: "For we shall all stand before the judgment seat of God" (Rom. 14, 10) or "So each of us shall give account of himself to God" (Rom. 14, 12). Christ himself sometimes makes God the judge, as in the parable of the merciful servant: "So also my heavenly Father will do to everyone of you, if you do not forgive your brethren from your heart" (Mt. 18, 35). In another text he describes himself as the advocate before the judgment seat of his Father: "So every one who acknowledges me before men, I also will acknowledge before my Father who is in heaven" (Mt. 10, 32). One explanation is that God is the supreme judge who has delegated the judgment to Christ and that Christ functions as a judge because he is the mediator of God's salvation.

The connection between the view of the Old Testament in which God himself passes the final judgment and the view of the New Testament in which Christ himself acts as a judge is expressed by Paul when speaking on the Areopagus he uses expressions which made the Athenians laugh: "The times of ignorance God overlooked, but now he commands all men everywhere to repent, because he has fixed a day on which he will judge the world in righteousness by a man whom he has appointed, and of this he has given assurance to all men by raising him from the dead" (Acts 17, 30-31).

Because Christ in the New Testament is seen as the judge at the end of time, it is understandable that the day of judgment, which was called the day of Yahweh, came to be called the day of Christ in the New Testament. There are several texts where the day of judgment is designated explicitly by this name: "who will sustain you to the end, guiltless in the day of our Lord Jesus Christ" (1 Cor. 1, 8). "I hope you will understand fully, as you have understood in part, that you can be proud of us as we can be of you, on the day of the Lord Jesus" (2 Cor. 1, 13-14). "Holding fast to the word of life, so that in the day of Christ I may be proud that I did not run in vain or labor in vain" (Phil. 2, 16).

The day of Christ is also understood in texts where this is not mentioned explicitly: "You are to deliver this man to Satan for the destruction of the flesh, that his spirit may be saved in the day of the Lord" (1 Cor. 5, 5). "For you yourselves knew well that the day of the Lord will come like a thief in the night" (1 Thess. 5, 2). Sometimes it is clear from the context that the expression "the day of the Lord" means the coming of Christ: "Now concerning the coming of our Lord Jesus Christ and our assembling to meet him, we beg you, brethren, not to be quickly shaken in mind or excited, either by spirit or by word, or by letter purporting to be from us, to the effect that the day of the Lord has come. Let no one deceive you in any way" (2 Thess. 2, 1-3).

Further, we can see that the Old Testament terms which indicated the "day of Yahweh" are now used to indicate the "day of Christ," such as: "the Day," "the great Day," "the Wrath" or "the day of Wrath." 'Each man's work will become manifest; for the Day will disclose it, because it will be revealed

with fire" (1 Cor. 3, 13). "And the angels that did
not keep their own position but left their proper
dwelling have been kept by him in eternal chains
in the nether gloom until the judgment of the
great Day" (Jude 1, 6). "But by your hard and
impenitent heart you are storing up wrath for yourself on the Day of wrath when God's righteous
judgment will be revealed" (Rom. 2, 5).

Even when sacred writers speak about "the day
of God" they mean "the day of Christ," as e.g.
in the 2nd letter of Peter the people are admonished:
"to be in lives of holiness and godliness, waiting
for and hasting the coming of the day of God" (3,
11-12). In the Acts we see that a prophecy of Joel
about the "day of Yahweh" is applied to Christ:
"the sun shall be turned into darkness and the moon
into blood, before the day of the Lord comes, the
great and manifest day. And it shall be that whoever
calls on the name of the Lord shall be saved" (2,
20-21). Christ himself saw the "day of Yahweh" and
"the day of Christ" as identical.

In the books of the New Testament Christ's being
a judge is considered in connection with his glorification, i.e. his death and resurrection. In the story
of Emmaus (Lk. 24, 13-35) we note that Christ
rebukes the two disciples because they did not
understand Holy Scripture: "O foolish men, and
slow of heart to believe all that the prophets have
spoken! Was it not necessary that the Christ should
suffer these things and enter into his glory?" We see

here that Christ's passion and death were a condition for his glorification.

We find the same thought expressed by Paul: "And being found in human form he humbled himself and became obedient unto death, even death on a cross. Therefore God has highly exalted him and bestowed on him the name which is above every name, that at the name of Jesus every knee should bow, in heaven and on earth and under the earth, and every tongue confess that Jesus Christ is Lord, to the glory of God the Father" (Phil. 2, 8-11). In another text Paul introduces the glorification of Christ in connection with his resurrection: "concerning his Son, who was descended from David according to the flesh and designated Son of God in power according to the Spirit of holiness by his resurrection from the dead, Jesus Christ our Lord" (Rom. 1, 3-4), and with his death and resurrection, when he says: "For to this end Christ died and lived again, that he might be Lord both of the dead and of the living" (Rom. 14, 9).

These statements may look strange to us, but nevertheless it is clearly stated in the New Testament that Christ was appointed as the Lord only at his resurrection; only at that moment was he appointed as the Son of God in power and as the Christ or Messiah (Acts 2, 36).

Of course Christ was the Son of God from the beginning. The angels announced him to the shepherds as Christ, the Lord; but at that moment he did not yet have these titles in the full sense of the word. During his earthly existence Christ was not the Lord, the Messiah and the Son of God in the full sense of these terms, because he did not yet exercise these functions. Only at his resurrection did he assume all the prerogatives of the Son of God, the Messiah and the Lord, because these dignities befit only a glorified person. Having been glorified by the Father in this way he could then assume these titles and could exercise his functions. Therefore we may say that only at his resurrection the Word which was made flesh came to full perfection. The resurrection is also called "the messianic enthronement" of Christ.

If we keep this in mind, we understand Paul when he says: "If Christ has not been raised, your faith is futile and you are still in your sins. Then those also who have fallen asleep in Christ have perished" (1 Cor. 15, 17-18). From these words we see that the death of Christ alone was not sufficient for our redemption: death and resurrection belong together. Even though they are not always mentioned together in the New Testament, still the authors are convinced that the two belong together. The resurrection is not necessarily taken as a proof, but it does show the reason why Christ, after it, can act as the redeemer. Only after his resurrection Christ can say: "All authority in heaven and on earth has been given to me" (Mt. 28, 18). After his resurrection "Lord" becomes the characteristic title for Christ.

This title "Lord" expresses his royal dignity, his sovereign power; it implies that Christ possesses all power. It is the title which was often given to Yahweh in the Old Testament.

THE EXPECTATION OF
CHRIST'S RETURN

In the Acts Luke mentions the last admonitions and promises of Christ to his disciples. Then he continues: "And when he had said this, as they were looking on, he was lifted up, and a cloud took him out of their sight. And while they were gazing into heaven as he went, behold, two men stood by them in white robes, and said: Men of Galilee, why do you stand looking into heaven? This Jesus, who was taken up from you into heaven, will come in the same way as you saw him go into heaven" (Acts 1, 9-11). The two men are heavenly beings, as is evident from their white garments. At the moment of Christ's departure the disciples receive the assurance from heaven that he will return. In this way his return is announced in the narrative of his departure; this we see also from the motif of the cloud: on a cloud he ascended, on a cloud he will descend.

It is evident from the books of the New Testament that the Christians expected Christ to return and that he would return as a judge. The entire New Testament prospect is dominated by this expectation. We might notice that never does it mention

his coming back, but merely his coming. This
method of expression indicates that "Christ's coming
at the end of time is a more original feature in the
books of the New Testament than his having come at
his incarnation."[1]

1. The Synoptic gospels

The gospels of Matthew, Mark and Luke are called
the synoptic gospels, because they are so much
alike. They reflect the early preaching and cate-
chesis. When speaking about his return, they always
allow Christ himself to speak. We may remark here
that there is evidently no reason to say that Christ
himself never spoke about his return, as if this
expectation were a creation of the first Christians
who put these words into his mouth. On the contrary,
we have reason enough to assert that the expectation
of his return, as much as the identification of the
day of Yahweh with the day of Christ, originates
from Christ himself.

So e.g. Lk. 17, 22-30 (cf. Mt. 24; 27, 37-39) are
considered as true words of Christ. "And he said
to the disciples: The days are coming when you will
desire to see one of the days of the Son of Man,
and you will not see it. And they will say to you:
Lo, there! or Lo, here! Do not go, do not follow
them. For as the lightning flashes and lights up the
sky from one side to the other, so will the Son of
Man be in his day. But first he must suffer many
things and be rejected by this generation. As it was
in the days of Noah, so will it be in the days of the
Son of Man. They ate, they drank, they married,

they were given in marriage, until the day when Noah entered the ark, and the flood came and destroyed them all. Likewise it was in the days of Lot — they ate, they drank, they bought, they sold, they planted, they built, but on the day when Lot went out from Sodom fire and brimstone rained from heaven and destroyed them all — so will it be on the day when the Son of Man is revealed." This text, both because of its form and of its contents, looks too original to be considered an invention of the Christian community. The title "Son of Man" for that matter is also an argument in favor of this, because, as we have said, only Christ himself uses this title; others never do.

The synoptic gospels speak very clearly about a glorious return of Christ at the end of time and about his coming as judge. This judgment is especially emphasized.

The best known text on this is the so-called "eschatological speech" (Mt. 24; Mk. 13; Lk. 21, 5-33), which is usually considered as referring to the last judgment. It may be good to substantiate this opinion briefly, because there are some who do not agree. (We follow the text of Matthew).

The following verses are the introduction: "Jesus left the temple and was going away, when his disciples came to point out to him the buildings of the temple. But he answered them: You see all these, do you not? Truly, I say to you, there will not be left here one stone upon another, that will not be thrown down. As he sat on the Mount of Olives, the disciples came up to him privately, saying: Tell us when will this be, and what will be the sign of your coming and of the close of the age?" (Mt. 24, 1-3; cf. Mk. 13, 1-4; Lk. 21, 5-7).

Instead of "the end of the world" the disciples say, literally, "the close of the age." This is a term from Jewish eschatology (cf. chapter I) and it is the same as that which we call "the end of this sinful world." In the parable of the weeds among the wheat (Mt. 13, 24-30, 36-40) this is very clear: The enemy who sowed them is the devil, the harvest is the close of the age, and the reapers are the angels (vs. 39). We see the same in the parable of the fish net (Mt. 13, 47-50): "So it will be at the close of the age. The angels will come out and separate the evil from the righteous" (vs. 49). And the same again is found in the words of Christ at the end of the gospel of Matthew: "And lo, I am with you always, to the close of the age" (28, 20). In all these passages the end of the world obviously is meant. Therefore we can translate it in this way.

From what the disciples said, it is evident that they meant the end of the world. According to Matthew the question is put in such a way to Christ that we may take it to be the intention of the gospel to speak about the end of the world.

Christ's manner of speaking about his coming also points in that direction. As Jewish eschatology places a period of distress before the messianic times, so also Christ speaks about a time of distress: "So when you see the desolating sacrilege spoken of by the prophet Daniel, standing in the holy place (let the reader understand), then let those who are in Judea flee to the mountains; let him who is on the housetop not go down to take what is in his house; and let him who is in the field not turn back to take his mantle. Pray that your flight may not be in winter or on a sabbath. For then there will be a great tribulation, such as has not been from the beginning of the world until now, and never will be. And if those days had not been shortened, no human being would be saved; but for the sake of the elect those days will be shortened. Then if any one says to you: Lo, here is the Christ! or: There he is! do not believe it. For false christs and false prophets will arise and show great signs and wonders, so as to lead astray, if possible, even the elect. Lo, I have told you beforehand. So, if they say to you: Lo, he is in the wilderness, do not go out; if they say: Lo, he is in the inner rooms, do not believe it. For as the lightning comes from the east and shines as far as the west, so will be the coming of the Son of Man. Wherever the body is, there the vultures will be gathered together" (Mt. 24, 15-28; cf. Mk. 13, 14-23; Lk. 17, 22-27).

In the verses 23-27 Christ warns his disciples about deceivers, false christs and false prophets. He says that there will be no doubt about the evidence of his coming. That the Messiah will come in secrecy, as the Jews say, is not true. Every one will be able to observe his coming, as every one notices the lightning in the sky.

The return itself is described by Christ as follows: "Immediately after the tribulation of those days the sun will be darkened, and the moon will not give its light, and the stars will fall from heaven, and the powers of the heavens will be shaken; then will appear the sign of the Son of Man in heaven, and then all the tribes of the earth will mourn, and they will see the Son of Man coming on the clouds of heaven with power and great glory; and he will send out his angels with a loud trumpet call, and they will gather his elect from the four winds, from one end of heaven to the other" (Mt. 24, 29-31; cf. Mk. 13, 24-27; Lk. 21, 25-27).

The way in which Christ describes his coming here agrees with the other descriptions of the end of the world and the last judgment. According to Matthew and Mark the angels collect the elect from the four winds. One can compare: "When the Son of Man comes in his glory, and all the angels with him, then he will sit on his glorious throne" (Mt. 25, 31); "For the Son of Man is to come with his angels in the glory of his Father, and then he will repay every man for what he has done" (Mt. 16, 27); "For whoever is ashamed of me and of my words in this adulterous and sinful generation, of him will the Son of Man also be ashamed, when he comes in the glory of his Father with the holy angels" (Mk. 8, 38; Lk. 9, 26). In all these texts the subject is undoubtedly the last judgment. We can add the explanations of the parables, already mentioned, of the weeds among the wheat and of the fish net, which as is said, mean the end of the world, and wherein also the angels play a role. So too the coming of the Son of Man on the clouds (Mt. 24, 30; Mk. 15, 26) is an indication that the end of the world is meant here. Finally there is the fact that first the gospel must be announced to all nations: "And this gospel of the kingdom will be preached throughout the whole world, as a testimony to all nations; and then the end will come" (Mt. 24, 14; Mk. 13, 10). All these texts of the synoptic gospels, which deal with the return of Christ at the end of time, justify the opinion that the eschatological speech also treats the same subject.

One might remark that the text of the eschatological speech does not give the impression that it is dealing with the last judgment of all men. The distress which is described (Mt. 24, 15-28; Mk. 13, 14-23; cf. our chapter XI) supposes that Judea is the scene of the events, not the whole world: in vs. 15 the desolating sacrilege is standing in the holy place (cf. our chapter XI) i.e. in the temple of Jerusalem; the mountains of vs. 16 are mountains of Judea, where fugitives often found refuge. Vs. 20 speaks about Jewish Christians who still keep the sabbath and do not walk farther than the allowed distance (about a mile). Moreover, the false prophets and the false christs form a Judean background (Mt. 24, 5; Mk. 13, 21-22). The persecution ("They will deliver you up to councils; and you will be beaten in syna-

gogues; and you will stand before governors and
kings for my sake, to bear testimony before them,"
Mk. 13, 9) supposes Palestine. We can also note that
the disciples asked: "Tell us when this will be,"
i.e. when will everything be destroyed? (Mt. 24, 2-3).

But we need not conclude from this that Christ
was speaking only about a historical event of Judea,
i.e. the fall of Jerusalem and the destruction of the
temple in 70 A.D. by the Romans. We can explain
this Judean background by the fact that the description originated in Palestine. It was in the tradition
of the Jewish Christians and the description was
adapted to their surrounding. The warnings assume
Palestinian surroundings, and because the Jews were
the great enemies and persecutors of the Christians,
they expected God's judgment to come upon the
Jews. They considered the last judgment a special
punishment for the Jews; this does not mean that
the last judgment was exclusively concerned with
Judea and the Jews. It is also understandable why
the disciples in their question made the last judgment and the destruction of the temple coincide.
The disciples believed that the kingdom of God and
the new world would begin only after the last judgment, when there would be an end to this sinful
world and to the enemies of Christ, especially the
Jews. We will speak more about this later (cf. pp.
77-92).

In speaking about the eschatological speech we
have already mentioned many passages from the
synoptic gospels which refer also to the coming of

Christ as judge. He comes with angels to punish the wicked and to collect the just. The wicked are those who do not accept him (Mt. 8, 38; Lk. 9, 26), sinners and evildoers (Mt. 13, 41), and those who are not merciful (Mt. 24, 44-45) etc. We will also speak again of this description of the last judgment (cf. pp. 65-73).

2. John

When compared to the synoptics John's gospel and his first letter show a vision of Christ's return which is quite different (cf. pp. 98-103). We find the same traditional anxiety for the return as in the synoptics. He too speaks about a coming of Christ as the judge at the end of time. The passages are not as frequent, as is to be expected in John, but in any case it is evident that he too knew the traditional view and accepted it.

When Christ is attacked by the Jews because of his cure on a sabbath, he defends himself by appealing to his Father and he says: "And he (the Father) has given him authority to execute judgment, because he is the Son of Man" (Jn. 5, 27). When John in his twelfth chapter speaks about the last and ineffectual warning of Christ to the Jews, he once more recapitulates everything which Christ has told them and he repeats the following words of Christ: "He who rejects me and does not receive my sayings has a judge; the word that I have spoken will be his judge on the last day" (Jn. 12, 48). In his first letter he writes: "And now, little children, abide in him, so that when he appears we may have confi-

dence and not shrink from him in shame at his
coming" (1 Jn. 2, 28).

From these passages it is evident that John holds
the general Christian belief that Christ as the Son
of Man is the judge of all. There is no reason to
consider, as later additions, the texts in which we
find this traditional opinion, as some scholars do.

3. Paul

When we read Paul's letters we notice how
often he reminds us that Christ will one day return
as the judge of living and dead, and that he will
judge everybody according to his works.

His two early letters, those to the Thessalonians
(the oldest writings of the New Testament) deal
chiefly with the return of Christ, because in Thessalonica difficulties had arisen concerning those faithful
who had already died before the return of Christ
(first letter). Next he deals with the question of
whether that return was near, as some of them
supposed (second letter).

In his other letters he speaks repeatedly about
the same subject and this can be explained only by
the fact that he was personally filled with desire to
be with Christ.

He knows that Christ will come as a judge. For
Onesiphorus who had been good to him he wishes:
"May the Lord grant him to find mercy from the
Lord on that day" (2 Tim. 1, 18). When he gives
admonitions to Timothy, he says: "I charge you in the

presence of God and of Christ Jesus who is to judge the living and the dead, and by his appearing and his kingdom: preach the word, be urgent in season and out of season, convince, rebuke and exhort, be unfailing in patience and teaching" (2 Tim. 4, 1-2). When he is criticized by the Corinthians he answers: "I am not aware of anything against myself, but I am not thereby acquitted. It is the Lord who judges me. Therefore do not pronounce judgment before the time, before the Lord comes, who will bring to light the things now hidden in darkness and will disclose the purposes of the heart. Then every man will receive his commendation from God" (1 Cor. 4, 4-5). Yet he awaits the judgment of Christ with great confidence. When he knows that he will soon die he writes to Timothy: "For I am already at the point of being sacrificed: the time of my departure has come. I have fought the good fight, I have finished the race, I have kept the faith. Henceforth there is laid up for me the crown of righteousness, which the Lord, the righteous judge, will award to me on that Day, and not only to me but also to all who have loved his appearing" (2 Tim. 4, 6-8).

This coming of Christ he keeps in mind constantly, and he reminds his readers often of it when he admonishes them to lead a Christian life and to practice virtue. So he writes to Titus: "For the grace of God has appeared for the salvation of all men, training us to renounce irreligion and worldly passions, and to live sober, upright, and godly lives in this world, awaiting our blessed hope, the appearing

of the glory of our great Lord and Savior Jesus
Christ, who gave himself for us to redeem us from
all iniquity and to purify for himself a people of his
own who are zealous for good deeds" (Tit. 2, 11-13).
To the Philippians he writes: "But our commonwealth is in heaven, and from it we await a Savior,
the Lord Jesus Christ, who will change our lowly
body to be like his glorious body, by the power which
enables him even to subject all things to himself"
(Phil. 3, 20-21). To the Colossians he writes: "If then
you have been raised with Christ, seek the things
that are above, where Christ is, seated at the right
hand of God. Set your minds on things that are
above, not on things that are on earth. For you
have died, and your life is hid with Christ in God.
When Christ who is our life appears, then you also
will appear in his glory" (Col. 3, 1-3).

These are but a few of the many examples which
we could point out in his letters.

4. James

James admonishes the Christians of Jewish origin
to be patient in the difficulties in which they find
themselves and he points out to them that the Lord
will come soon to give everybody his deserved reward. "Be patient, therefore, brethren, until the
coming of the Lord. Behold, the farmer waits for
the precious fruit of the earth, being patient over
it until it receives the early and the late rain. You
also be patient. Establish your hearts, for the coming
of the Lord is at hand. Do not grumble, brethren

against one another, that you may not be judged; behold the Judge is standing at the doors" (Jas. 5, 7-9).

We notice that he too considers the coming of Christ as a judgment.

5. Peter

In the first letter of Peter the expectation of the return takes an important place. The sufferings which we must bear are alleviated by the certainty of the reward which we will receive when Christ returns: "Beloved, do not be surprised at the fiery ordeal which comes upon you to prove you, as though something strange were happening to you. But rejoice insofar as you share Christ's sufferings, that you may also rejoice and be glad when his glory is revealed" (4, 12-13). In the same vein at the beginning of his letters he says: "In this you rejoice, though now for a little while you may have to suffer various trials, so that the genuineness of your faith, more precious than gold which though perishable is tested by fire, may redound to praise and glory and honor at the revelation of Jesus Christ" (1, 6-7).

In his second letter he warns his Christians against those who laugh at the return. The author however holds fast to his belief: "For we did not follow cleverly devised myths when we made known to you the power and coming of our Lord Jesus Christ, but we were eye-witnesses of his majesty" (1, 16). For this belief he appeals to the transfiguration which he considers an anticipation of the return, to the word of the prophets and to a number of facts which may be a sign for the unbelievers that the Lord will certainly return.

6. The Book of Revelation

Revelation, an eminently apocalyptic book, is devoted entirely to the subject of Christ's return. Though it does not speak exclusively about this subject, yet it breathes the expectation of the coming of Christ. The Son of Man in 1, 13 is the glorified Christ, the eschatological judge, the same as in Dan. 7, 13, who returns at the end of time to judge the godless. "Behold, he is coming with the clouds, and every eye will see him, every one who pierced him; and all tribes of the earth will wail on account of him. Even so. Amen" (1, 7). "He who testifies to these things says: Surely I am coming soon! Amen! Come, Lord Jesus!" (22, 20).

5

THE RESURRECTION

We have already seen (p. 11) that from the second century B.C. there was an expectation of a general resurrection of the dead which would precede the judgment. This judgment would be truly universal.

The New Testament, too, knows about a resurrection which will precede the last judgment. However, this resurrection is not mentioned as often as is the return. In the Catholic letters e.g. we find no mention of it. We may remark that the universal resurrection of sinners, together with the just, is but seldom mentioned. In most cases we find reference made only to the resurrection of the just. We should not be astonished by this unilateral view. It does not mean that the authors did not know a resurrection of sinners; it shows only that the resurrection of the just had their principal attention. For the just only is it a real resurrection, because they will enter into life; for the sinners it means only a second death.

The synoptic gospels speak often about a resurrection. We have e.g. the dispute of Christ with the Sadducees about this subject (Mt. 22, 23-33; Mk. 12, 18-27; Lk. 20, 27-40). Christ's answer is: "You are

ou know neither the Scriptures nor
od. For in the resurrection they
r are given in marriage, but are
heaven. And as for the resurrection
, ... you not read what was said to you
by God, I am the God of Abraham, and the God of
Isaac, and the God of Jacob? He is not God of the
dead, but of the living" (Mt. 22, 29-32). Luke mentions once more, explicitly, a resurrection of the
just: "But when you give a feast, invite the poor,
the maimed, the lame, the blind, and you will be
blessed, because they cannot repay you. You will
be repaid at the resurrection of the just" (Lk. 14,
13-14). Beyond this we find nothing.

It is remarkable that none of the synoptics speaks
about resurrection in connection with the return of
Christ, which shows that this connection was not
thought of in the early Christian tradition. This may
be explained by the fact that the Christians during
these years lived in the expectation that this return
would take place during their lifetime. They knew
about a general resurrection, but this did not concern
them, as they thought. Therefore they probably paid
less attention to this point.

When however, after some years, many Christians
had died, there arose an uneasiness, at least in
Thessalonica. They were anxious about the fate of
their deceased and they were afraid that these would
not get their full share with the other faithful.

Because of these difficulties Paul in his first letter
speaks to the Thessalonians: "But we would not

have you ignorant, brethren, concerning those who are asleep, that you may not grieve as others do who have no hope. For since we believe that Jesus died and rose again, even so, through Jesus, God will bring with him those who have fallen asleep. For this we declare to you by the word of the Lord, that we who are alive, who are left until the coming of the Lord, shall not precede those who have fallen asleep. For the Lord himself will descend from heaven with a cry of command, with the archangel's call, and with the sound of the trumpet of God. And the dead in Christ will rise first; then we who are alive, who are left, shall be caught up together with them in the clouds to meet the Lord in the air and so we shall always be with the Lord. Therefore comfort one another with these words" (4, 13-18).

In this letter Paul spoke about the resurrection to remove the worries of the Christians. Shortly afterward he was forced to defend his teaching specifically against a certain Greek mentality. We notice in the first letter to the Corinthians, there were some who did not believe in the resurrection of the body: "Now if Christ is preached as raised from the dead, how can some of you say that there is no resurrection of the dead?" (15, 12). The Greeks were averse to a resurrection of the body; the body was the prison of the soul and the sooner the soul could be liberated from this prison the better. In Corinth there were Christians who held the same opinion. Against them Paul asserts that there will be a resurrection and that the resurrection of Christ proves that such a resurrection is possible. If even the resurrection of Christ were denied, our faith would be worthless, because all expectation of God's salvation is based upon this resurrection (cf. pp. 23-25).

In his other letters he often mentions the resurrection: "Since we have the same spirit of faith as he who wrote: I believed, and so I spoke, we too believe and so we speak, knowing that he who raised the Lord Jesus will raise us also with Jesus and bring us with you into his presence" (2 Cor. 4, 13-14). "That I may know him and the power of his resurrection, and may share his sufferings, becoming like him in his death, that if possible I may attain the resurrection from the dead" (Phil. 3, 10-11).

John too mentions a resurrection of the dead on the last day. In his speech at Capharnaum Christ says: "This is the will of him who sent me, that I should lose nothing of all that he has given me, but raise it up at the last day" (6, 39). "No one can come to me unless the Father who sent me draws him; and I will raise him up at the last day" (6, 44). According to John the resurrection concerns the sinners as well as the just: "The hour is coming when all who are in the tombs will hear his voice and come forth, those who have done good, to the resurrection of life, and those who have done evil, to the resurrection of judgment" (5, 28-29). Revelation speaks about a resurrection of the just and the unjust: "And the sea gave up the dead in it, Death and

Hades gave up the dead in them, and all were judged by what they had done . . . And if any one's name was not found written in the book of life, he was thrown into the lake of fire" (20: 13, 15).

There must be a resurrection because a body is necessary for a truly human life.

6

REWARD ACCORDING TO MERITS

With regard to the return and the judgment it is often said in the New Testament that Christ will judge everyone according to his deeds. In line with the current expectation it is also said that those who have lived virtuously will enter into the kingdom of God and that those who have done evil will be excluded from it. We find no systematic exposition about the fate of the just and the sinners. Reward and punishment are often mentioned, but are described in various ways. These descriptions imply that the reward of the just will be great happiness and the punishment of the sinners will be deep misery. All this is described in a manner which may appeal to us as human beings.

Christ preferably described the happiness of the just in figures of earthly joys. Their happiness in the kingdom of God is described as a banquet or a nuptial feast: "I tell you, many will come from east and west and sit at the table with Abraham, Isaac and Jacob in the kingdom of heaven" (Mt. 8, 11; cf. Lk. 13, 29). "I tell you I shall not drink again of this fruit of the vine until that day when I drink it new with you in my Father's kingdom"

(Mt. 26, 29). In the parables the happiness of the
kingdom of God is compared to a banquet: "The
kingdom of God may be compared to a king who
gave a marriage feast for his son" (Mt. 22, 2). The
parable of the unwilling guests: "A man gave once
a great banquet and invited many" (Lk. 14, 16). The
parable of the foolish and the wise maidens: "And
while they went to buy, the bridegroom came, and
those who were ready went in with him to the marriage feast; and the door was shut" (Mt. 25, 10).
Previously, the prophets liked to describe the joys
of the messianic age as a banquet: "On this mountain
(Zion) the Lord of hosts will make for all peoples
a feast of fat things, a feast of wine on the lees, of
fat things full of marrow, of wine on the lees well
refined" (Is. 25, 6). Christ uses these popular metaphors.

This happiness is also compared to a treasure:
"If you would be perfect, go, sell what you possess
and give to the poor, and you will have a treasure
in heaven" (Mt. 19, 21). "Lay up for yourselves
treasures in heaven" (Mt. 6, 20). It is depicted as
a great reward: "Rejoice and be glad, for your
reward is great in heaven" (Mt. 5, 12). Or it is
called, simply, the life: "It is better for you to enter
life maimed than with two hands to go to hell"
(Mk. 9, 43). Life means here **the** life, a life which is
not troubled by sadness, suffering or death. Of
course this life is eternal.

This idea goes beyond earthly descriptions.

In the letters of the New Testament the reward

of the just is pictured as something that brings joy: "But rejoice insofar as you share Christ's sufferings, that you may also rejoice and be glad when his glory is revealed" (1 Pet. 4, 13). Or it is depicted as honor and glory: "Glory and honor and peace for every one who does good" (Rom. 2, 10).

Besides these passages which describe the reward of the just as great happiness, as honor and glory, there are others which say what it is we shall enjoy. The just will be united with Christ: "And so we shall always be with the Lord" (1 Thess. 4, 17). "Now concerning the coming of our Lord Jesus Christ and our assembling to meet him, we beg you, brethren . . ." (2 Thess. 2, 1). They will be with Christ in heaven: "And raised us up with him, and made us sit with him in the heavenly places in Christ Jesus" (Eph. 2, 6). They will be with Christ in the house of the Father: "In my Father's house are many rooms; if it were not so, would I have told you that I go to prepare a place for you?" (Jn. 14, 2).

They will see God: "Beloved, we are God's children now; it does not yet appear what we shall be, but we know that when he appears we shall be like him, for we shall see him as he is" (1 Jn. 3, 2). "Now I see in a mirror dimly, but then I will see face to face. Now I know in part; then I shall understand fully, even as I have been fully understood" (1 Cor. 13, 12).

They do not explain how this "seeing God" must be understood, but John gives the impression of the reward of the just in his Revelation: "Then I saw a new heaven and a new earth; for the first heaven and the first earth had passed away, and the sea was no more. And I saw the holy city, new Jerusalem, coming down out of heaven from God, prepared as a bride adorned for her husband; and I heard a great voice from the throne saying: Behold, the dwelling of God is with men. He will dwell with them, and they shall be his people, and God himself will be with them; he will wipe away every tear from their eyes, and death shall be no more, neither shall there be mourning nor crying nor pain any more, for the former things have passed away. And he who sat upon the throne said: Behold, I make all things new. Also he said: Write this, for these words are trustworthy and true. And he said to me: It is done! I am the Alpha and the Omega, the beginning and the end. To the thirsty I will give water without price from the fountain of the water of life. He who conquers shall have his heritage, and I shall be his God and he shall be my son" (21, 1-7). This is the way in which John depicts eternal happiness.

"It seems preferable to picture the heaven of the Christians to ourselves as the new Jerusalem, the paradise of God, and the nuptials of the Lamb, as John describes them in Revelation, rather than as an academy of speculating spirits, as sometimes described in theological treatises. The desire of modern man to save the earth and its life is based upon an authentic Christian nostalgia."[2]

This heavenly bliss, according to our theology, consists chiefly in seeing God and is certainly the most important aspect of it. But we may never forget that it is likewise to be a human happiness in which our body will share. Therefore some propose to compare the final fulfillment to the life which Christ was leading here on earth when he saw the Father and worked on earth: "In this case eternal bliss would be at the same time very heavenly and very earthly."[3] Or with a little addition: "The life of our Lord on earth is very much similar to our beatitude, but his glorified life is the real authentic type of that beatitude. He operates no more in an earthly sense, while at the same time there is the joyful excitement of a banquet."[4]

The fate of the sinners is depicted as extreme misery. Jesus pictures it as a condition of sorrow and hopelessness, because they have definitely lost happiness. "There you will weep and gnash your teeth, when you see Abraham and Isaac and Jacob and all the prophets in the kingdom of God and you yourselves thrust out" (Lk. 13, 28). It is depicted as being excluded from the nuptial banquet as the five foolish maidens were excluded by the bridgegroom (Mt. 25, 12). Or as being cast into the outer darkness: "And cast the worthless servant into the outer darkness; there men will weep and gnash their teeth" (Mt. 25, 30). Darkness is here opposed to the light within the banquet room and it reminds us of the darkness of the underworld.

The misery of sinners is not described merely negatively as deprivation of eternal happiness; it is also considered positively as a punishment. This punishment is depicted as a condemnation. The punishment allotted to the bad servant by his master is: "and will punish him" (Mt. 24, 51). "But as for those enemies of mine, who did not want me to reign over them, bring them here and slay them before me" (Lk. 19, 27). Their punishment consists in the loss of life.

The punishment which is mentioned most often in the synoptic gospels is the punishment of fire, the fire of the hell: literally the fire of the Gehenna.

The name "Gehenna" is derived from the valley of Hinnom near Jerusalem. Because of the abominations which were practised there, the offering of children to Moloch, Jeremiah announces that God will hold a judgment over Israel in this place; there will be many corpses, so many that they cannot be buried (Jer. 7, 31; 8, 2). In this way this valley came to be considered as a place of execution. When Isaiah describes the new time of God's favor, the valley of Hinnom is the place where the corpses of the apostates will be eaten by the worms or burned by the fire (Is. 66, 24). In the second century B.C. the Jews picture the valley of Hinnom as a valley full of fire in which at the end the Jewish apostates will be punished: but now no longer only their corpses, but they themselves living in the body. After some time, Gehenna no longer was spoken of in connection with the valley of Hinnom; it simply meant the place where sinners were punished by fire and as such it is described in the New Testament.

Christ takes over these Jewish figures of the punishment of sinners. "But I will warn you whom to fear: fear him who, after he was killed, has power to cast into hell (Greek: **Gehenna**)" (Lk. 12, 5). "And if your eye causes you to sin, pluck it out and throw it from you; it is better for you to enter life with one eye than with two eyes to be thrown into the hell (Greek: Gehenna) of fire" (Mt. 18, 9).

This Gehenna is also meant when the furnace of fire is mentioned: "The Son of Man will send his angels, and they will gather out of his kingdom all causers of sin and all evildoers, and throw them into the furnace of fire; there men will weep and gnash their teeth" (Mt. 13, 41-42). Or when the eternal fire is mentioned: "Then he will say to those at his left hand: Depart from me, you cursed, into the eternal fire prepared for the devil and his angels" (Mt. 25, 41). The unquenchable fire: "If your hand causes you to sin, cut if off; it is better for you to enter life maimed than with two hands to go to hell, to the unquenchable fire" (Mk. 9, 41-42). The Baptist uses the same figure: "His winnowing fork is in his hand, to clear his threshing floor, and to gather the wheat into his granary, but the chaff he will burn with unquenchable fire" (Lk. 3, 17). So too John in Revelation: "Then Death and Hades were thrown into the lake of fire, this is the second death, the lake of fire; and if any one's name was not found written in the book of life, he was thrown into the lake of fire" (20, 14-15). "But as for the cowardly, the faithless, the polluted, as for murderers, fornicators, sorcerers, idolaters, and all liars, their lot shall be in the lake that burns with fire and brimstone, which is the second death" (21, 8).

When according to Mark (9, 47-48) Jesus says: "And if your eye causes you to sin, pluck it out; it is better for you to enter the kingdom of God with one eye than with two eyes to be thrown down into hell, where their worm does not die, and the fire is not quenched," then this worm is reminiscent of the description which Isaiah gave of the valley of Hinnom as the place of execution for the apostates, whose corpses were lying there unburied; the words "where their worm does not die and the fire is not quenched," for that matter, are a quotation of Is. 66, 24.

Outside the synoptic gospels the punishment of sinners is sometimes called "death": "For the wages of sin is death" (Rom. 6, 23). This death is not the death of the body but a spiritual death. It is the counterpart of life. It is the absolute absence of happiness, the being deprived of God's love. This is what Revelation calls the second death (20, 14; 21, 8), which is worse than the death of the body.

This punishment is also called destruction: "They shall suffer the punishment of eternal destruction and exclusion from the presence of the Lord and from the glory of his might" (2 Thess. 1, 9). It is also called the wrath of God: "He who does not obey the Son shall not see life, but the wrath of God rests upon him" (Jn. 3, 36). According to John and every one who understands what God means, this is the worst lot which can befall a man: to have incurred disgrace in the sight of God, who is the supreme good and the supreme love.

7

THE END

In his first letter to the Corinthians Paul writes: "Then comes the end, when he delivers the kingdom to God the Father after destroying every rule and every authority and power. For he must reign until he has put all his enemies under his feet. The last enemy to be destroyed is death. For God (Greek: he) has put all things in subjection under his feet. But when it says: All things are put in subjection under him, it is plain that he is excepted who put all things under him. When all things are subjected to him, then the Son himself will also be subjected to him who put all things under him, that God may be everything to every one" (1 Cor. 15, 24-28).

The things about which Paul speaks here are those which are inimical to the kingdom of God. Christ's task is to destroy these powers. As long as this has not yet happened Christ must reign, i.e. exercise his kingship fighting them. At his return all these will be destroyed; death too, the last enemy, shall be overcome. Then Christ will no longer have to exercise his kingship by fighting these powers: then "the Son himself will also be subjected to him who put all things under him," Paul says, and this remark of his appears somewhat strange to us.

It means simply that at the end Christ will have performed his redemptive duty and that accordingly he will report to his Father that he has carried out his mission, and at the same time he will transfer to his Father the reign over all men whom he has gathered under himself as their head. Then all creatures will be subject to God.

This subjection of Christ does not mean that the divine and the human nature would not still be united: Christ remains the God-man, he remains also king and Lord, "only his combatant kingship has come to an end, as also in general that aspect of his mediatorship which made it necessary that separate acts of Christ and his servants were needed to fill the gap between the Father and us."[5]

8

THE MILLENNIUM

The expectation of a millennary reign is first met in later Judaism; though we must remark at once that this expectation was not adhered to by all without exception. In the beginning the messianic times were identified with the future world, the reign of God. But about the second century we notice that in certain writings a distinction is made: the messianic time becomes then an intermediate reign which precedes the general judgment. It is then a reign which has its place in this world and is characterized by great earthly and spiritual happiness. It is the summit and at the same time the end of this world.

Although according to the usual Jewish opinion the resurrection could take place only at the last judgment, we notice in certain circles toward the end of the second century A.D. an expectation that the deceased saints and martyrs will also have their share in the messianic times and that consequently they would rise.

About the duration of the messianic reign, opinions are very divergent; they vary from some decades to many thousands of years. In connection with the

week of creation some preferred to divide the history
of the world into seven millennia. To the six days
in which God created the world there would be six
thousand years in which the history of mankind had
its course. God's resting on the seventh day has its
parallel in the heavenly rest which the just will
enjoy during a thousand years, in expectation of the
last judgment and the fulfillment of all. This last
millennium is then considered the messianic reign.
This division into periods of a thousand years probably has its origin in the Persian eschatology; those
who adhered to this expectation were called "chil-
iasts" or "millennarians."

After the fall of Jerusalem in 70 A.D. this **chiliasm**
had a strong revival in Jewish circles. It is for this
reason that it also had followers among the Christians. A text of Revelation, which was interpreted
incorrectly, was a great influence in this respect.
We read there: "Then I saw an angel coming down
from heaven, holding in his hand the key of the
bottomless pit and a great chain. And he seized
the dragon, that ancient serpent, who is the Devil
and Satan, and bound him for a thousand years, and
threw him into the pit, and shut it and sealed it
over him, that he should deceive the nations no more,
till the thousand years were ended. After that he
must be loosed for a little while. Then I saw
thrones, and seated on them were those to whom
the judgment was committed. Also I saw the souls
of those who had been beheaded for their testimony
to Jesus and for the word of God, and who had not

worshiped the beast or its image and had not received its mark on their foreheads or their hands. They came to life, and reigned with Christ a thousand years. The rest of the dead did not come to life until a thousand years were ended. This is the first resurrection. Blessed and holy is he who shares in the first resurrection! Over such the second death has no power, but they shall be priests of God and of Christ and they shall reign with him a thousand years" (20, 1-6). In the passage which follows this we find a description of Satan who is liberated again from his shackles and for the last time militates against the people of God. But he is cast down into the pool of fire. Then follow the general resurrection and the last judgment (20, 7-15).

It can hardly be denied that this description was inspired by the Jewish expectation of the millennium with which the author was familiar. In the course of the history of Christianity this text of Revelation has often been interpreted literally, i.e. that Christ will return once more to this earth. Then, at his return, the martyrs will rise, or even all the just, and they will reign with Christ during a thousand years on this earth. The earth will be changed into a paradise, where there is an abundance as never has been. After this follow the general resurrection, the last judgment and the coming of the kingdom of heaven.

From the second to the fourth century there were many Christians who followed this chiliasm. One

of the first, who is well known, is the heretic Cerin-
thus, who went so far as to describe the paradisic
world of the millennium as an enjoyment of all
earthly joys, even the most carnal ones. Besides
him there were also many fathers of the Church,
ecclesiastical writers and bishops such as Papias,
Justin, Irenaeus, Tertullian, Hippolytus, Methodius of
Olympus, Appolinaris of Laodicaea and others. Their
good faith usually cannot be doubted. At this time
however it was a disputed doctrine, against which
other fathers of the church and ecclesiastical writers
argued fiercely. One such was Origen, who pointed
out that Revelation should be understood allegori-
cally. His disciple St. Dionysius of Alexandria dealt
a heavy blow to chiliasm. The official creeds of the
Church have never alluded to this doctrine. Another
reaction against chiliasm was that doubts arose against
the divine inspiration of Revelation. After the fourth
century this doctrine was no longer held.

The general panic which arose around the year
1000 A.D. because of the opinion that the end of
the world was near proved that thoughts about the
millennium had not entirely died down. In the
twelfth century the Abbot Joachim of Fiore caused
a temporary revival of chiliasm. Using Revelation
he gave a new interpretation of history as a soteri-
ological development. In it he distinguished three
periods: the first one was the period of God the
Father, the second of God the Son and the third of
God the Holy Spirit. This last period would, according to him, commence in the year 1260 and

would last till the end of time, the time of the
"eternal gospel" (Rev. 14, 6). This gospel was not a
written book, but the spiritual understanding of the
Old and New Testament. The letter of Christ's
gospel and the Church of clerics and sacraments
would pass away. The Church would be spiritual-
ized, a new contemplative order would preach the
eternal gospel in order to remedy the corruption of
the world.

In more recent times several sects have breathed
new life into chiliasm; such are the Anabaptists of
the 16th century and, in our time, the Mormons, the
Adventists and the Witnesses of Jehovah. This last
sect, which attracts much attention by its activity,
expects mankind to last 6000 years, after which the
millennium will follow. This millennial reign is the
central part of their doctrine. By a rather whimsical
interpretation of the Bible, Russell, its founder, expected the invisible return of Christ in the year
1874, after which followed a harvest time of forty
years, during which only a small part of the then
living people could choose between eternal life and
eternal perdition. The beginning of the millennium
would be in 1914. This is a decisive time in which
the souls of the deceased are awakened from their
sleep in order to make a choice. Those who make
a good choice receive an eternal life in this world;
the unrepentant will be destroyed. In the year 2914
there will be a new heaven and a new earth.

During the second world war a moderate chiliasm

found some adherence even among Catholics. A decree of the holy Office of July 21, 1944, declared however that this could not be taught safely, because it accepts two returns and two resurrections.

Chiliasm has never been condemned formally by the Church; neither has theology marked it as heretical, but it certainly is an error. Nothing forces us to interpret Revelation literally. On the contrary, this book usually expresses itself in symbols. Augustine was in favor of a spiritual interpretation of Rev. 20, 7-15. He compared this passage with Jn. 5, 24-29. Here John distinguishes a double resurrection: the first one when man hears the word of God and believes in it, a spiritual resurrection; and a second one, bodily, at the end of time when the dead rise up from their graves. Therefore Augustine proposes the resurrection about which Rev. 20, 1-6 speaks as the spiritual resurrection of those who receive life, because they accept the doctrine of Jesus. Many scholars have taken over this interpretation and consider the millennium as the time of the Church which lasts from the first Pentecost till the end of time.

Still another interpretation of this passage is possible. We can understand it symbolically, since all the visions of Revelation are symbolic. In this connection it is useful to pay attention to the considerable influence which Ezekiel exercised on the thoughts of the author of Revelation. Now, in Ezek. 37, 1-14 we find a description of dry bones

which come to life. This symbolizes the people of
Israel who after the national downfall and the
Babylonian captivity will be restored again. This
vision is followed immediately by the description of
a great attack on the holy land by Gog, who on this
occasion is destroyed by God, so that Israel could
live in peace (Ezek. 38-39). In Revelation we see that
after the first resurrection and the millennium there
follows immediately an attack of Satan and of Gog
and Magog. This justifies the opinion that the first
resurrection is a symbol of the revival of the Church
after a period of bloody persecution. The millennium would thus be a symbol of the earthly period
of the Church, beginning with the Roman persecutions and lasting till the end of time.

Further we should notice that in the rest of the
New Testament there is no trace whatsoever of
chiliasm. The return of Christ will coincide with the
last judgment at the end of time. There are some
non-catholic scholars who put some stress on a
double resurrection, one of the faithful and one of
the others, between which they place the millennium.
For this opinion they appeal to 1 Cor. 15, 22-25:
"For as in Adam all die, so also in Christ shall all
be made alive. But each in his own order: Christ
the first fruits, then at his coming those who belong
to Christ. Then comes the end, when he delivers the
kingdom to God the Father after destroying every
rule and every authority and power. For he must
reign until he has put all his enemies under his
feet." Instead of "after this comes the end" they

translate however "after this comes the rest," i.e. the rest of mankind; this translation however is purely arbitrary.

9

THE DECOR OF CHRIST'S RETURN

In the New Testament we find many dramatic descriptions of Christ's return. These have often been interpreted as a realistic report of the events to happen. But really they are, as we shall see, only the accepted figures of the prophets and the apocalyptics. This should teach us not to pay so much attention to the accidental features, as to neglect the essential. The descriptions of the coming of Christ serve to explain the importance of this coming.

The most important truth which is taught in these passages is this: our own actions are decisive for our future fate. When Christ comes he will judge every one according to his deeds.

1. The Synoptic Gospels

The appearance of Christ in the synoptics is accompanied by cosmic upheavals. Mark describes these in the same way as Matthew: "But in those days, after that tribulation, the sun will be darkened, and the moon will not give its light, and the stars will be falling from heaven, and the powers in the heavens will be shaken" (Mk. 13, 24-25; Mt. 24-29;

cf. p. 30-31). The powers of heaven are the sun, moon and stars. The description of Luke is somewhat different: "And there will be signs in sun and moon and stars, and upon the earth distress of of nations in perplexity at the roaring of the sea and the waves, men fainting with fear and with foreboding of what is coming on the world; for the powers of the heavens will be shaken" (Lk. 21, 25-26).

We should remember that these are very familiar metaphors derived from the prophetic literature. When the prophets describe the day of Yahweh, they use the same figures of speech. When they describe God's intervention in history, heaven and earth become involved. The darkening and falling of the stars especially are often mentioned among these cosmic terrors. Thus Amos says: "And on that day, says the Lord God, I will make the sun go down at noon, and darken the earth in broad daylight" (8, 9). "That day" is the day of Yahweh. Isaiah describes it as follows: "Behold, the day of the Lord comes, cruel, with wrath and fierce anger, to make the earth a desolation and to destroy its sinners from it. For the stars of the heavens and their constellations will not give their light, the sun will be dark at its rising and the moon will not shed its light" (13, 9-10). "All the host of heavens shall rot away, and the skies roll up like a scroll. All their host shall fall, as leaves fall from the vine, like leaves falling from the fig tree" (34, 4). Joel uses the same figures describing the day of Yahweh:

"Multitudes, multitudes, in the valley of decision! For the day of the Lord is near in the valley of decision. The sun and the moon are darkened, and the stars withdraw their shining" (3, 14-15). Or: "The sun shall be turned into darkness, and the moon to blood, before the great and terrible day of the Lord comes" (3, 4). What has given rise to these figures of speech are natural phenomena, such as moon — and sun eclipses (the reddish brown color makes people think of blood), and falling stars which terrified primitive man. We meet these figures in the apocalyptic writings too; here these natural phenomena are even amplified to show that God's judgment causes great changes in the history of mankind.

The New Testament copies these descriptions. In Revelation we find them return when the day of wrath is announced: "When he opened the sixth seal, I looked, and behold, there was a great earthquake; and the sun became black as sackcloth, the full moon became like blood, and the stars of the sky fell to the earth as the fig tree sheds its winter fruit when shaken by a gale; the sky vanished like a scroll that is rolled up, and every mountain and island was removed from its place. Then the kings of the earth and the great men and the generals and the rich and the strong, and every one, slave and free, hid in the caves and among the rocks of the mountains, calling to the mountains and rocks: Fall on us and hide us from the face of him who is seated on the throne, and from the wrath of the Lamb,

for the great day of their wrath has come, and who
can stand before it?" (6, 12-17). One can see that
the author here imitates the prophets, e.g. the
prophecy against Edom (Is. 34, 4), hiding in the
caves (Is. 2, 10), calling to the mountains and to
the rocks: Fall upon us (Hos. 10, 8; Lk. 23, 30). We
notice the similarity with the synoptics when this
description is used to depict impressively the terrific
character of God's wrath.

The descriptions in the synoptics must be interpreted in the same way. Christ uses figures of speech
which were familiar from the Bible. The cosmic
upheavels are not a sign of the return of Christ:
they are simply its decor. They are not events
which will take place, but symbols which help
give us an impression of the terrifying character of
the day of the Lord (cf. Mt. 24, 30: "Then all the
tribes of the earth will mourn.")

We have already remarked (p. 27) that in Acts
1, 11 the return of Christ is expected as a coming
on the clouds of heaven. In the synoptics we find
this several times: "And then they will see the Son
of Man coming in clouds wtih great power and
glory" (Mk. 13, 26; Mt. 24, 30; Lk. 21, 27). This is
the way in which Christ announces his return to
his disciples. Before Caiaphas he gives a similar
description of his coming: "I am; and you will see
the Son of Man sitting at the right hand of Power,
and coming with the clouds of heaven" (Mk. 14, 62;
Mt. 26, 64). Revelation announces him with these
words: "Behold, he is coming with the clouds" (1, 7).

These descriptions must be understood as symbols, not as literally described events. The coming upon the clouds of heaven evidently refers to Dan. 7, 13-14 (cf. p. 12). This vision symbolizes the establishment of the kingdom of God at the end of time, following the conquering of world powers which are inimical to God. It is obvious that Christ, using this symbol, wishes to express a similar thought: the triumph of the kingdom of God. His return means that he and his people, his faithful, will triumph over all the powers which are against them.

The presence of angels at Christ's return is also to be understood as a symbol. We have mentioned on page 30 a number of passages from the synoptic gospels where angels are mentioned. In the letters of Paul to the Thessalonians we find this decor: the archangel's call (1 Thess. 4, 16; cf. page 43); "When the Lord Jesus is revealed from heaven with his mighty angels in flaming fire" (2 Thess. 1, 7). Sometimes the angels are the companions of Christ (Mt. 16, 27; 25, 31), at other times they are witnesses at the judgment (Lk. 12, 8), or they summon the people (1 Thess. 4, 16; Mt. 24, 31; Mk. 13, 27). That the angels are with Christ is stressed. The angels belong to the royal court of God. If they have the same function toward Christ as they have toward God, this implies the heavenly character of Christ.

The trumpet which is mentioned in Mt. 24, 31 and 1 Thess. 4, 16, is also heard in the description of the day of Yahweh: "And in that day a great trumpet will be blown, and those who were lost in the land of Assyria and those who were driven out to the land of Egypt will come and worship the Lord on the holy mountain at Jerusalem" (Is. 27, 13). "Blow the trumpet in Zion; sound the alarm on my holy mountain! Let all the inhabitants of the land tremble, for the day of the Lord is coming, it is near" (Joel 2, 1). The Jewish and rabbinic writings repeated this trumpet call. It was also a familiar feature to the Jews.

We have already mentioned several symbolic elements in the description of the coming of Christ. Our next question is: What are we to think about the judgment of Christ?

The procedure of this judgment is described extensively in Mt. 25, 31-46: "When the Son of Man comes in his glory, and all the angels with him, then he will sit on his glorious throne. Before him will be gathered all the nations, and he will separate them one from another as a shepherd separates the sheep from the goats, and he will place the sheep at his right hand, but the goats at the left. Then the King will say to those at his right hand: Come, O blessed of my Father, inherit the kingdom prepared for you from the foundation of the world; for I was hungry and you gave me food, I was thirsty and you gave me drink, I was a stranger and you welcomed me, I was naked and you clothed me, I was sick and you visited me, I was in prison and you came to me. Then the righteous will answer him: Lord, when did we see thee hungry and feed

thee, or thirsty and give thee drink? And when did
we see thee a stranger and welcome thee, or naked
and clothe thee? And when did we see thee sick
or in prison and visit thee? And the king will answer
them: Truly, I say to you, as you did to one of the
least of these my brethren, you did it to me. "Then
he will say to those at his left hand: Depart from
me, you cursed, into the eternal fire prepared for
the devil and his angels; for I was hungry and you
gave me no food, I was thirsty and you gave me
no drink, I was a stranger and you did not welcome
me, naked and you did not clothe me, sick and in
prison and you did not visit me. Then they also
will answer: Lord, when did we see thee hungry
or thirsty or a stranger or naked or sick or in
prison, and did not minister to thee? Then he will
answer them: Truly, I say to you, as you did it not
to one of the least of these, you did it not to me. And
they will go away into eternal punishment, but the
righteous into eternal life."

The judgment of Christ is described here as a
trial takes place in our experience: the judge on
his seat, the persons to be judged (here all men),
the trial, the separation of the guilty and the inno-
cent, and finally the verdict.

These features must be considered only as a
graphic description. In reality the judgment must be
seen in a different way.

The judgment takes place during the life of man,
when he freely accepts Christ or rejects him: "He

who believes in him is not condemned; he who does
not believe is condemned already, because he has
not believed in the name of the only Son of God"
(Jn. 3, 18). In this life man develops an attitude
toward God, either of love or aversion. Thus at a
man's death his future fate has already been decided.
Through resurrection man is restored again to his
full human existence; therefore it will depend on his
attitude toward God, the attitude in which he has
lived, how this resurrection will be; considered in
this way, the resurrection itself is the judgment,
"Do not marvel at this; for the hour is coming when
all who are in the tombs will hear his voice and
come forth, those who have done good, to the resurrection of life, and those who have done evil, to
the resurrection of judgment" (Jn. 5, 28-29).

According to our doctrine about individual judgment, we are judged at our death: at that moment
our soul receives the reward or the punishment which
our actions deserve. We know that the last judgment
will not change anything: it only corroborates it.

The Bible speaks only of the general judgment.
It looks at man as a whole, body and soul, and
therefore the requittal man receives for his actions
is placed in the general judgment at the return of
Christ, because only at that moment do we again
have the entire man. The judgment at Christ's
return is not a spectacular trial; essentially it means
that at the moment of resurrection those who have
lived justly will enter into God's kingdom; and that

those who have sinned will be excluded from this kingdom: this is the separation.

Therefore, we should not interpret the New Testament literally when we read that the faithful at Christ's return will be judges with him: this is a biblical way of speaking. "Do you not know that the saints will judge the world" means only that the just man, united to Christ, will acknowledge that the just merits his reward and that the sinner deserves his punishment.

2. Peter

In the second letter of Peter we find another description of Christ's return: "But the day of the Lord will come like a thief and then the heavens will pass away with a loud noise, and the elements will be dissolved with fire, and the earth and the works that are upon it will be burned up. Since all those things are thus to be dissolved, what sort of persons ought you to be in lives of holiness and godliness, waiting for and hastening the coming of the day of God, because of which the heavens will be kindled and dissolved, and the elements will melt with fire. But according to his promise we wait for new heavens and a new earth in which righteousness dwells" (3, 10-13).

The author expects a renewal of the universe. His idea is also connected with prophetic tradition: "For as the new heavens and the new earth which I will make shall remain for me, says the Lord; so shall your descendants and your name remain" (Is. 66, 22).

"For behold, I create new heavens and a new earth;
and the former things shall not be remembered or
come into mind" (Is. 65, 17). Among the Jews this
expectation of a cosmic renewal was very common
and we find it returning in the New Testament as
we see here and also in Matthew, where a "regen-
eration" is mentioned (19, 28), i.e. a renewal. In
the same sense in Acts 3, 21 we hear about "estab-
lishing all things." Revelation describes "a new
heaven and a new earth; for the first heaven and
the first earth have passed away" (21, 1).

According to the second letter of Peter the old
world will be burned by fire. This idea is found
in the Old Testament. Perhaps we may point to
Zephaniah: "Neither their silver nor their gold shall
be able to deliver them on the day of the wrath of
the Lord. In the fire of his jealous wrath, all the
earth shall be consumed; for a full, yea, sudden end
he will make of all the inhabitants of the earth"
(1, 18) or: "Therefore wait for me, says the Lord,
for the day when I arise as a witness. For my decision is to gather nations, to assemble kingdoms, to
pour out upon them my indignation, all the heat
of my anger; for in the fire of my jealous wrath
all the earth shall be consumed" (3, 8). These texts
are evidently entirely metaphoric.

In the late-Jewish apocalypses and also in one
of the Psalms of thanksgiving discovered near the
Dead Sea we find the idea of a world conflagration.
Probably the idea came to the Jews from the world

of the Greeks, though the origin may lie farther back. It could be accepted easily, because in the Old Testament the judgment of God is sometimes represented as an annihilating fire, as we saw in the above quoted passages of Zephaniah and of Isaiah: "For behold, the Lord will come in fire, and his chariots like the stormwind, to render his anger in fury, and his rebuke with flames of fire. For by the fire will the Lord execute judgment, and by his sword, upon all flesh" (66, 15-16).

With this description of the world conflagration the author of the letter does not mean to teach that the world will really be consumed by fire at the end, as one might conclude from these passages. This world fire is a figure of the day of the Lord. He intends to teach us that Christ in his glory will come to judge at the moment he chooses. This will be the end of the world. The worldwide conflagration is merely a way of showing that the return of Christ means the end of this sinful world and that then a new world, a new time of righteousness will dawn. The world fire is merely a dramatic way of describing it.

3. Revelation

As for the description which Revelation gives of Christ's return, the very name of the Book is a warning that we should not take these descriptions too literally. Revelation makes use of symbols, and these express only that the kingdom of God shall one day come, that previously there will be a struggle between good and evil, but that by the return of Christ evil will be overcome. The dead will rise and be judged according to their merits. Those who have sinned receive eternal punishment and those who have lived justly receive an eternal reward: in the kingdom of God they receive eternal happiness with God.

In whatever way the return of Christ is described in the New Testament, it always shows that Christ will be victorious and that he will bring the end of history.

10

THE MOMENT OF
CHRIST'S RETURN

1. The Proximity of Christ's Return

As we read the New Testament, we get the impression that the first Christians lived in the expectancy of a proximate coming of Christ on the clouds.

In the second letter to the Thessalonians we read the following admonition of Paul: "Now concerning the coming of our Lord Jesus Christ and our assembling to meet him, we beg you, brethren, not to be quickly shaken in mind or excited, either by spirit or by word, or by letter purporting to be from us, to the effect that the day of the Lord has come. Let no one deceive you in any way" (2, 1-3). From this passage it is obvious that around 51 A.D. in Thessalonica at least there were Christians who expected the return of Christ to take place in the near future. We see the same in the second letter of Peter: "First of all you must understand this, that scoffers will come in the last days with scoffing, following their own passions and saying: Where is the promise of his coming? For ever since the fathers fell asleep, all things have continued as they were from the beginning of creation" (3, 3-4). As this letter was written between 70 and 80 A.D., it is evident that the expectation of an imminent return was still alive at that time, because the delay of the visible victorious return had caused some people to abandon their belief in such a return. This letter is a reaction to these unbelieving scoffers.

From this reaction of Paul and of the author of the second letter of Peter we may not conclude that they did not share this expectation. Paul warns here only against those people who had stopped working with a view to an imminent return of Christ.

In his letters there are clear indications that he himself also reckoned with a possibility that Christ might appear soon. The passage in his first letter to the Thessalonians where he speaks about the resurrection (4, 13-18) can be considered as a proof of this, because he says: "We who are alive, who are left until the coming of the Lord" (4, 15). So the passage in the first letter to the Corinthians: "Lo! I tell you a mystery. We shall not all sleep, but we shall all be changed" (15, 51). But it may also be that Paul in an oratorical way of speaking only places himself and the Thessalonians among those who are still alive at the return of Christ, as in another text he places himself among the dead: "And God raised the Lord and will also raise us up by his power" (1 Cor. 6, 14).

There are other passages which show that he did expect an imminent return of Christ: "Besides this you know what hour it is, how it is full time now for you to wake from sleep. For salvation is nearer to us now than when we first believed; the night is far gone, the day is at hand" (Rom. 13, 11). "Rejoice in the Lord always; again I will say: Rejoice. Let all men know your forbearance. The Lord is at hand. Have no anxiety about anything" (Phil. 4, 4-6).

The author of the second letter of Peter attempts to explain why the return is delayed. He points to Psalm 90, 4 as proof: "For a thousand years in thy sight are but as yesterday when it is passed, or as a watch in the night." God does whatever he has promised but if his return has not yet taken place this shows that God looks at time in a manner which is different from ours. In things divine we should not count in days of twenty-four hours. If Christ's return is delayed the reason is not God's dilatoriness, but his longanimity: "The Lord is not slow about his promises as some count slowness, but is forbearing towards you, not wishing that any should perish, but that all should reach repentance" (2 Pet. 3, 9). The writer stresses the uncertainty of the moment of the return, but he does not reject the expectation of an imminent return. On the contrary, he suggests that a righteous life may accelerate the return and he admonishes his readers to look forward to it with great desire: "waiting for and earnestly desiring the coming of the day of God" (2 Pet. 3, 12).

In other writings of the New Testament we find

indications that a near-at-hand return of Christ was
being reckoned with: "You also be patient. Establish
your hearts, for the coming of the Lord is at hand"
(Jas. 5, 8). "The end of all things is at hand; therefore keep sane and sober for your prayers" (1 Pet.
4, 7). "He who testifies to these things says: Surely
I am coming soon! Amen! Come, Lord Jesus" (Rev.
22, 20).

The synoptics mention words of Christ which give
the impression that his coming on the clouds would
take place before the death of the then-living generation: the so called terminal texts. These passages
(we take them all from Matthew) are: "When they
persecute you in one town, flee to the next; for
truly, I say to you, you will not have gone through
all the towns of Israel, before the Son of Man
comes" (10, 23). "Truly, I say to you, there are
some standing here who will not taste death before
they see the Son of Man coming in his kingdom"
(16, 28; cf. Mk. 8, 39; Lk. 9, 27), "Truly, I say to you,
this generation will not pass away till all these things
take place" (24, 34). "Jesus said to him (Caiaphas):
You have said so. But I tell you, hereafter you
will see the Son of Man seated at the right hand of
Power, and coming on the clouds of heaven" (26, 64).

We may assume that Christ's preaching about his
return, and especially his manner of expression in
speaking of it, must have given his disciples the impression that his return in glory would not be long
delayed. It must have created many problems for
the early Christians, when he did not return. The

synoptic gospels still show traces of the uneasiness. As a result exegetes in our days are still confronted with such problems.

In connection with these pronouncements of Christ many opinions have been brought forward, some admissible, some not. Some assert that Christ lived in the illusion that the kingdom of God would come soon, during his lifetime and before his disciples had finished their missionary journeys during his public life. For this they point to the passage of Mt. 10, 23, which we quoted above. This expectancy of Christ failed to materialize and therefore he comes to the conclusion that the new age must be brought about through penance and through the sacrifice of his life. Others say that Christ never had the idea of a glorious return in mind. The first Christians created this expectancy.

Christian scholars reject such opinions and look for another solution to the problem, without however coming to an agreement.

To remove such problems by denying that there is question of an early return in these texts has often been tried. The apostles, they say, never had such an expectation. This is proved by the pronouncements of Christ about the absolute uncertainty of the moment his return would take place. When Christ is asked just before his ascension: "Lord, will you at this time restore the kingdom to Israel?" he answers: "It is not for you to know times or seasons which the Father has fixed by his own authority"

(Acts 1, 7). Speaking in his eschatological speech about his coming, he remarks: "But of that day or that hour no one knows, not even the angels in heaven, nor the Son, but only the Father" (Mk. 13, 32; cf. Mt. 24, 36). It may seem strange to us that Christ declares that he himself does not know the moment of his return, but the very difficulty which this verse creates for us is a proof for its authenticity. Christ here does not speak about his divine knowledge, because being God he knows everything. Here he speaks only about his human knowledge. If we consider this as acquired knowledge, as our knowledge is, he could "increase in wisdom" (Lk. 2, 52) and possibly there are things he does not know. As a man he received from his Father an insight into everything which concerned his mission; consequently whatever he does not know is of no importance for his mission.

This explanation, according to which nobody needed to know when the return would take place, makes it sufficiently clear that in the above quoted texts there is no question about a near-at-hand return. In confirmation of this they point to the command of Christ to preach the gospel to all nations. In his eschatological speech Christ said: "And this gospel of the kingdom will be preached throughout the whole world, as testimony to all nations; and then the end will come" (Mt. 24, 14; Mk. 13, 10). After his resurrection he appeared to his disciples and said: "All authority in heaven and on earth has been given to me. Go therefore and make disciples

of all nations, baptizing them in the name of the
Father and of the Son and of the Holy Spirit,
teaching them to observe all that I have commanded
you; and lo, I am with you always, to the close of
the age" (Mt. 28, 18-20; cf. Mk. 16, 15; Lk. 24, 47).
Such a command seems irreconcilable with the assertion that the end is near. The behavior of the
apostles in this regard does not give us the impression that they expected the end to come soon.

Moreover these scholars draw our attention to
some parables which speak about the return which
insinuate that this return may be delayed. Such is
the parable of the maidens: "Then the kingdom of
heaven shall be compared to ten maidens who took
their lamps and went to meet the bridegroom. Five
of them were foolish and five were wise. For when
the foolish took their lamps, they took no oil with
them, but the wise took flasks of oil with their
lamps. As the bridegroom was delayed, they all
slumbered and slept. But at midnight there was a
cry: Behold, the bridegroom! Come out to meet
him! Then all those maidens rose and trimmed
their lamps. And the foolish said to the wise:
Give us some of your oil, for our lamps are going
out. But the wise replied: Perhaps there will not be
enough for us and for you: go rather to the dealers
and buy for yourselves. And while they went to
buy, the bridegroom came, and those who were
ready went in with him to the marriage feast and
the door was shut. Afterward the other maidens
came also, saying: Lord, lord, open to us. But he

replied: Truly, I say to you, I do not know you. Watch therefore, for you know neither the day nor the hour" (Mt. 25, 1-13). "Let your loins be girded and your lamps burning, and be like men who are waiting for their master to come home from the marriage feast, so that they may open to him at once when he comes and knocks. Blessed are those servants whom the master finds awake when he comes; truly, I say to you, he will gird himself and have them sit at table, and he will come and serve them. If he comes in the second watch or in the third, and finds them so, blessed are those servants" (Lk. 35-38). "But know this, that if the householder had known at what hour the thief was coming, he would have been awake and would not have left his house to be broken into. You also must be ready; for the Son of Man is coming at an hour you do not expect" (Lk. 12, 39-40).

All these arguments, however, with which these scholars corroborate their opinion that in these passages Christ does not speak about an imminent return, are not very much to the point.

The fact that the precise moment is unknown does not exclude the possibility that it could be expected to happen soon. There is as much reason to think that it may happen soon as to think that it may be delayed. Moreover, the uncertainty does not so much concern the question whether such return is nearby or far off; but it does concern the sudden-ness of its occurence. This is proved by the context in which the texts of Mt. 24, 36 and of Mk. 13, 32

occur. In Matthew we are referred to the time of
Noah, when the Flood took people by surprise. Mark
adds: "Take heed, watch; for you do not know when
the time will come. It is like a man going on a
journey, when he leaves home and puts his servants
in charge, each with his work, and commands the
doorkeeper to be on the watch. Watch therefore —
for you do not know when the master of the house
will come, in the evening, or at midnight, or at
cockcrow, or in the morning — lest he come sud-
denly and find you asleep. And what I say to you
I say to all: Watch" (Mk. 13, 33-37). Comparison is
made with a thief in the night (cf. above Lk. 12,
39-40) as pointing to a sudden and unforeseen return.

Other authors of the New Testament use this
simile to exhort their readers to vigilance. "But as
to the times and the seasons, brethren, you have no
need to have anything written to you. For you
yourselves know well that the day of the Lord will
come like a thief in the night. When people say:
There is peace and security, then sudden destruction
will come upon them as travail comes upon a woman
with child, and there will be no escape" (1 Thess.
5, 1-3). "But the day of the Lord will come like a
thief" (2 Pet. 3, 10). "If you will not awake, I will
come like a thief, and you will not know at what
hour I will come upon you" (Rev. 3, 3). What
sense could such exhortations have, if there were
only a negligible chance of being taken by surprise?
The insistence of these admonitions shows that the
possibility of a sudden return is very real.

Therefore the disciples were of the opinion that not much time would elapse between Christ's departure and return. The delay of his coming, which is hinted at in the parables, they considered relatively short. The time to preach the gospel must, in their opinion, have been very short. The inhabited world, for that matter, was in their eyes much smaller than the world today. As for the activity of the disciples, we may not forget that as time went on, their thoughts must have changed.

There are some indications from which we may conclude that the pronouncement of Christ which mention a certain term were understood in connection with his return. Matthew 10, 23 places the admonitions of Christ to his disciples at the moment he was sending them on a small missionary journey among the Jews (Mt. 10, 1-42). However in vs. 23 there is a statement which does appear out of context. It follows after this passage: "Beware of men; for they will deliver you up to councils, and flog you in their synagogues, and you will be dragged before governors and kings for my sake, to bear testimony before them and the Gentiles. When they deliver you up, do not be anxious how you are to speak or what you are to say; for what you are to say will be given to you in that hour; for it is not you who speak, but the Spirit of your Father speaking through you. Brother will deliver up brother to death, and the father his child, and children will rise against their parents and have them put to death; and you will be hated by all for my name's sake, but he who endures to the end will be saved" (10, 17-22). This passage supposes a time of persecutions; at the moment Jesus was sending out his apostles on that journey, conditions were not so serious. As it is, we see that in the gospel of Mark and Luke these words of Jesus are placed in his eschatological speech, where Matthew himself repeats this passage once more in a shortened form (cf. Mt. 24, 9-13; Mk. 13, 9-13; Lk. 21, 12-19). This shows that this verse must be interpreted in connection with Christ's return. Mt. 16, 28 follows a verse which certainly is about the return: "For the Son of man is to come with his angels in the glory of his Father, and then he will repay every man for what he has done." After this we find: "Truly, I say to you," . . . etc.

Seeing all this we are forced to say that Christ wanted to teach his disciples that in a certain way he would come during their lifetime. The disciples and the first Christians however applied this to his visible coming at the end of time.

As this is no matter of doctrine we may hold that the apostles and early Christians thought that his return at the end of the world would not be long delayed. One cannot however say that Christ, the apostles and the authors of the New Testament taught this, because this would mean that they affirmed something which is not true and this is incompatible with their infallibility.

Another solution of the problem is possible.

2. Proposed solution

The best solution to this problem is to suppose that the expectation of the return underwent an evolution. In the beginning this expectation was very much influenced by Old Testament and apocalyptic ideas: contemporary ideas also exercised a great influence.

In his preaching Christ spoke the language of his time, as we can see in the gospel. When speaking about his return he expressed himself in terms with which the people of his time were familiar. These ideas were taken from the Old Testament and apocalyptic writings. Thus he speaks about his return and the judgment as "**the** Day": "On that day many will say to me: Lord, Lord, did we not prophesy in your name, and cast out demons in your name, and do many mighty works in your name," etc. (Mt. 7, 22). He speaks about "this world" and "the future world": "And whosoever says a word against the Son of Man will be forgiven: but whoever speaks against the Holy Spirit will not be forgiven, either in this age or in the age to come" (Mt. 12, 32). "There is no one . . . who will not receive a hundredfold now in this time, houses, and brothers and sisters and mothers and children and lands, with persecutions, and in the age to come eternal life" (Mk. 10, 30). Speaking in the style of the prophets and the apocalyptics he expressed his thoughts in language familiar to the people. The apocalyptics described it in such a way as if this evil age, this sinful world, would come to an end on the Day

of Yahweh, a day of judgment; then begins a new
age, a world in which righteousness reigns. The
new or future world follows after this world. When
Jesus speaks about this world or the future world,
his words give the impression that one follows after
the other and that "the Day" is placed on the
boundary between them.

Nevertheless the present age and the future one
lie partly side by side. The resurrection of Christ
is already the beginning of the future world; but
the present world continues till the moment Christ
will close it at the fulfillment of the age (Mt. 28, 20).
Therefore the Day must be understood differently
from the way it was described in the prophets and
the apocalyptic writings. In fact, the Day began
with the glorification of Christ and it lasts till the
end of this world. From this we must conclude that
the Day or the Day of Christ is not one of twenty-
four hours. It would even be better not to consider
it as something which denotes time. The Day of
Yahweh was meant chiefly to express God's intervention in history; so also the Day of Christ must
be understood as the intervention of Christ in history. At his resurrection Christ began to lead this
world to its fulfillment. At that moment the world
entered into its last period: we are at present living
in the end of time.

Considered in this light, which shows us the
real situation, we can more easily understand Christ's
prounouncements that the then-living generation
would witness his return. We have already seen

that Christ was vested with all this power through his resurrection. At that moment he was appointed a judge, and since his resurrection he acts as a judge. When he speaks about his coming we should not think primarily of a coming in a visible manner, but of a coming by means of certain events which would be revelation of the triumphant Christ. Even in the Old Testament we see that certain events which were thought of as helping or punishing intervention were considered as a coming of God. In the same manner we can see every triumph and every punishment of Christ as a coming.

So also in the passages in which Christ describes his coming as an event which will happen in the near future we must think of some manifestation of Christ, either by punishing the Jew (Mt. 10, 23; 24, 34), or by the triumph of Christianity (Mt. 16, 28; 26, 64). Consequently we can say that such comings of Christ cannot be chronologically identified with his return at the end of time when he will close history. Theologically however they constitute one coming. If we consider all these as one coming, we take a truly more correct view.

Having gained a better insight into the delay of the final coming of Christ and into the intricacy of the mystery of the parousia, theology today knows successive parousias: the one of the judgment of Jerusalem, the one which takes the Church by surprise in each of her members and finally the parousia of the end. But it is arbitrary to make these distinctions in the texts themselves. The texts speak

only about the coming of Christ, but we know this
to be multiple in its manifestations; all these manifestations are, in themselves and in the thought of
Christ, one.[6]

It is quite understandable that the disciples of
Christ concluded from his words that he would return soon and that the end of the world was near.
They were living in the world of Old-Testament
and apocalyptic ideas. Therefore they understood
his words in this spirit. The coming of Christ was
for them a coming to close this world and to inau-
gurate the new one; moreover, they pictured this
coming according to the descriptions of the apocalyptic writings as an event with much pomp and
show.

In all phenomena, especially in the resurrection
of Christ, they saw a sign that the end of time was
drawing near. Therefore they also expected him to
return soon on the clouds, and they looked forward
toward it with great desire. But he did not appear.
In the beginning they were disappointed, but as
time went on, this delay of a visible return proved
very instructive for them. It made them reflect on
things. They began to understand that the pomp
and show was of no significance, but that the
triumph of Christ's spirit was. Then came the understanding that the glorification of Christ and his
salutary activity constituted the end of time. Moreover they gained a better understanding of the importance of the eschatological favors which Christ
was giving them henceforth; they learned to pay

attention to his coming into their souls. The tense expectation with which they had been looking forward to his imminent visible coming eased. A subsiding of this tension can be traced in the writings of the New Testament.

3.   Later reflections

When we read the synoptics we notice that the early Christians looked forward very eagerly to the moment when Christ would come back in a glorious manifestation, and this in the near future. In Matthew this is even more manifest than it is in Mark.

(I)   Mt. 16, 28 says: "Truly, I say to you, there are some standing here who will not taste death before they see the Son of Man coming in his kingdom."

(II)   In Mt. 24, 29, after the description of the great distress we read: "**Immediately** after the tribulation of those days the sun will be darkened, and the moon will not give its light, and the stars will fall from heaven, and the powers of the heavens will be darkened" etc. and after this follows the description of the return.

(III)   In Matt. 26, 64 Jesus answers the question of Caiaphas: "You have said so. But I tell you, **hereafter** you will see the Son of Man seated at the right hand of Power, and coming on the clouds of heaven."

These passages in Mark read as follows:

(I)   Mk. 8, 39: "Truly, I say to you, there are some

standing here who will not taste death before they see the kingdom of God come with power."

(II) Mk. 13, 24: "But in those days, after that tribulation, the sun will be darkened" etc.

(III) Mk. 14, 62: "And Jesus said: I am; and you will see the Son of Man sitting at the right hand of Power and coming with the clouds of heaven."

Compared with these two evangelists Luke's texts are remarkable:

(I) Lk. 9, 27: "But I tell you truly, there are some standing here who will not taste death before they see the kingdom of God."

(II) Lk. 21, 24 interposes between the distress and the return "the times of the Gentiles."

(III) Lk. 22, 69: "But from now on the Son of Man shall be seated at the right hand of the power of God."

Luke is remarkable in that he purposely tempers some of Jesus' sayings in such a way so that less attention is drawn to the proximity of his return. Probably he did this because as time went on the return evidently was delayed.

The three of them describe the return in apocalyptic colors.

In Paul's letters we find an evident evolution of his eschatology. In his first letters we notice a vivid expectation of the return; in his later letters this

expectation still turns up regularly, but we see that
more and more he stresses the effects of salvation
which have already been realized in us, and upon
the Church and its significance for salvation.

In his two earliest letters, written to the Thessalonians, which are so important for us because of
their eschatology, we see that Paul's attention is
entirely concentrated upon the resurrection of Christ
and upon his return in glory. At his return all those
who have believed in him will receive the effect of
his salvation, including those who will have died
before his coming (1 Thess. 4, 13-18; cf. p. 69).
The way he describes the return is apocalyptic in
style, as it is in the synoptics. We have already
drawn attention to this fact (pp. 69-71). In these
letters he often makes use of the traditional vocabu-
lary of the apocalyptics; the judgment is a day of
wrath for the enemies of Christ (1 Thess. 2, 16), an
avenging judgment. We find an example of this
in the first chapter of the second letter: "Since
indeed God deems it just to repay with affliction
those who afflict you, and to grant rest with us to
you who are afflicted. (And this will be) when the
Lord Jesus is revealed from heaven with his mighty
angels in flaming fire, inflicting vengeance upon
those who do not know God and upon those who do
not obey the gospel of our Lord Jesus. They shall
suffer the punishment of eternal destruction and
exclusion from the presence of the Lord and from
the glory of his might, when he comes on that day
to be glorified in his saints, and to be marveled at

in all who have believed, because our testimony to you was believed" (2 Thess. 1, 6-10).

Not only the terms and the descriptions, but even the tone of his words has an Old Testament and apocalyptic ring. These letters are pervaded by this expectancy; everything looks toward the future. These letters date from the year 51 A.D.

In his letters to the Corinthians we notice first of all that Paul has not dropped this expectation. This is especially obvious in the instructions about the resurrection (1 Cor. 15) and also in such passages as: "So that you are not lacking in any spiritual gift, as you wait for the revealing of our Lord Jesus Christ, who will sustain you to the end, guiltless in the day of our Lord Jesus Christ" (1 Cor. 7-8). "Each man's work will become manifest; for the Day will disclose it, because it will be revealed with fire, and the fire will test what sort of work each one has done" (1 Cor. 3, 13).

The end is depicted as a final battle in the spirit of the apocalyptic writings: Christ will put all his enemies under his feet (1 Cor. 15, 25). He will destroy every rule and every authority and power (1 Cor. 15, 24). But at the same time we see also that apocalyptic descriptions are giving way to a more rational discussion to explain the resurrection in order to make it acceptable to the Greeks (1 Cor. 15).

In these letters we note that Paul, along with his expectation of the future, also stresses the reality which is present. Christian life does not consist only in an expectancy of future union with Christ; by faith and baptism we have already been united with him. The faithful are already in Christ. "Do you not know that your bodies are members of Christ?" (1 Cor. 6, 15). "He who is united to the Lord becomes one spirit with him" (1 Cor. 6, 17). "Do you not know that your body is a temple of the Holy Spirit within you?" (1 Cor. 6, 19). We also see the same juxtaposition of expectation of the future and of consciousness of what has already been realized in his letters to the Romans, Galatians and Philippians: "For in this hope we were saved. Now hope that is seen is not hope. For who hopes for what he sees? But if we hope for what we do not see, we wait for it with patience" (Rom. 8, 24-25). "I am sure that he who began a good work in you will bring it to completion at the day of Jesus Christ" (Phil. 1, 6).

Further we read: "For we know that Christ being raised from the dead will never die again, death no longer has dominion over him. The death he died he died to sin, once for all, but the life he lives he lives to God. So you also must consider yourselves dead to sin and alive to God in Christ Jesus" (Rom. 6, 9-11). "For I know that through your prayers and the help of the Spirit of Jesus this will turn out for my deliverance" (Phil. 1, 19). We are in possession of the promised Spirit, but somewhat in the manner of an handsel (a down-payment on something we hope to get): we still hope for the complete realization. "We ourselves, who have the first fruits of the Spirit, groan inwardly as we wait for adoption as sons, the redemption of our bodies" (Rom. 8, 23). These letters to the Corinthians, Romans, Philippians, Galatians date from the years 56-58 A.D.

Later, during his first captivity (61-63), when Paul writes his letters to the Colossians and Ephesians there is a remarkable shift in his perspective. He now stresses the realized eschatology. In the first letter to the Corinthians he was still waiting for the complete victory of Christ: "He must reign until he has put all his enemies under his feet" (1 Cor. 15, 25). In Ephesians he writes: "And he has placed all things under his feet" (1, 22). The victory is considered realized, because ". . . he disarmed the principalities and powers and made a public example of them, triumphing over them in it (i.e. the cross)" (Col. 2, 15); the victory is referred back to the death and resurrection.

Paul told the Christians of Thessalonica (1 Thess. 4, 16) that they would rise at Christ's return. In the letters to the Colossians and the Ephesians he points out that their resurrection has already been realized. They now share in the victory of Christ. God has "made us alive together with Christ" (Eph. 2, 5). "You were buried with him in baptism, in which you were also raised with him, through faith in the working of God, who raised him from the dead" (Col. 2, 12). God has "delivered us from the dominion of darkness and transferred us to the kingdom of his beloved Son, in whom we have redemption, the forgiveness of sins" (Col. 1, 13-14).

In the letter to the Ephesians Paul draws special attention to the Church as the body of Christ: "And he (God) has put all things under his feet and has made him the head over all things for the church, which is his body, the fullness of him who fills all in all" (Eph. 1, 22-23). This stress upon the realized eschatology does not mean that he is no longer interested in the future. The expectation has not vanished entirely from his letters. "And do not grieve the Holy Spirit of God, in whom you were sealed for the day of redemption" (Eph. 4, 30). "When Christ who is our life appears, then you also will appear with him in glory" (Col. 3, 4). The return of Christ at the end of time is only the finishing touch to the triumph; victory itself has already been achieved now.

In Revelation when the millennium is mentioned (20, 1-6), it is considered a bridging of the gap between Christ's departure and his return (cf. pp. 57-64).

In this evolution of the expectation of the return, the gospel of John constitutes a summit. It was written toward the end of the first century.

If we compare the eschatology of John with that of the synoptics and the other books of the New Testament it seems as if we enter into an entirely new world of ideas. We find no apocalyptic descriptions as we did in the synoptics: the coming

of the Son of Man on the clouds is not mentioned,
there is no description of the last judgment. From
this we may not conclude however that John dropped
this traditional eschatology as we described it in our
chapter IV. We have already pointed out that John,
in several places of his gospel, shows that he knows
and accepts that traditional view. We must therefore say that he puts more stress upon the other
aspects of the eschatology, viz. on eschatology insofar as it is already present, insofar as it has already
been realized. Traditional eschatology was chiefly
concerned with the expectation of the return of
Christ, the resurrection and the judgment inasmuch
as these still lie in the future. John however puts
stress upon an eschatology already realized in the
faithful. He shows that the expectation of the
traditional eschatology concerning the return of
Christ has already reached reality in those who
believe in Christ. According to him we do not
partake of these eschaltological favors only on the
last day. They have been given to us now as a gift,
as a possession which cannot be lost. We see this
in such texts as: "He who believes in the Son has
eternal life; he who does not obey the Son shall
not see life, but the wrath of God rests upon him"
(3, 36). "Truly, truly, I say to you, he who hears my
word and believes him who sent me, has eternal life;
he who does not come into judgment, but has passed
from death to life. Truly, truly, I say to you, the
hour is coming, and now is, when the dead will
hear the voice of the Son of God, and those who
hear will live" (Jn. 5, 24-25). The dead are those

who are spiritually dead. "He who believes in him is not condemned; he who does not believe is condemned already, because he has not believed in the name of the only Son of God" (Jn. 3, 18). "Truly, truly, I say to you, he who believes has eternal life" (Jn. 6, 47). "I am the living bread which came down from heaven; if any one eats of this bread, he will live for ever" (Jn. 6, 51). Eating of this bread is a metaphor for believing in Christ. "Truly, truly, I say to you, if any one keeps my word, he will never see death" (Jn. 8, 51). "But you do not believe, because you do not belong to my sheep. My sheep hear my voice, and I know them, and they follow me; and I give them eternal life, and they shall never perish, and no one shall snatch them out of my hand" (Jn. 10, 26-28).

Reception of the Holy Eucharist also has this effect: "He who eats this bread will live for ever" (Jn. 6, 58). When we study such passages as: "This is the will of my Father, that every one who sees the Son and believes in him should have eternal life; and I will raise him up at the last day" (Jn. 6, 40), or: "He who eats my flesh and drinks my blood has eternal life, and I will raise him up at the last day" (Jn. 6, 54), we see that the eternal life which we receive through faith and through reception of the Holy Eucharist are distinguished from the resurrection on the last day.

From this it is evident that according to John the judgment takes place in this life, when a man accepts Christ or rejects him; and that eternal life is a gift which we receive when we believe in and partake of the Eucharist.

The return of Christ realizes itself in this life according to Jn. 14, 1-24. In different ways, Christ reveals his spiritual presence. His return (vs. 3) consists in the following: 1. His disciples continue his work: "He who believes in me will also do the works that I do; and greater works than these will he do" (vs. 12). 2. The Holy Spirit will dwell in them: "If you love me, you will keep my commandments. And I will pray the Father, and he will give you another Counselor, to be with you for ever, even the Spirit of truth, whom the world cannot receive, because it neither sees him nor knows him, you know him, for he dwells with you, and will be in you" (vs. 15-17). 3. The disciples will see him in a spiritual way: "Yet a little while, and the world will see me no more, but you will see me; because I live, you will live also" (vs. 19). 4. There will always be a bond of love: "He who has my commandments and keeps them, he it is who loves me, and he who loves me will be loved by my Father, and I will love him and manifest myself to him" (vs. 21). The real return consists in the exchange of divine love: "If a man loves me, he will keep my word, and my Father will love him, and we will come to him and make our home with him" (vs. 23).[7]

In 16, 16-22 we see such an interpretation of the return. The words of Jesus: "A little while, and you will see me no more; again a little while, and you will see me" (16, 16) are explained by Jesus in such

a way as to show that he returns at the resurrection.
John sees the return of Christ as a spiritual coming
which persists in those who believe in him.

But, as we have said repeatedly, John does not
forget the traditional idea about the return and the
glorious resurrection. He attempts to teach the doctrine of Christ, as well as the synoptics. But he
emphasizes such aspects as have not yet had attention or not sufficiently so, viz. that a Christian now
has part in the divine life in a real, though imper-
fect way. Only at the general resurrection will he
receive this life in its fullness. The traditional eschatology therefore has not become superfluous for him:
bodily resurrection is the necessary fulfillment of
the eternal life we possess now.

The first letter of John is akin to the fourth gospel
in regard to this question. There too we find the
anticipated eschatology: "Children, it is the last
hour; and as you have heard that the antichrist
is coming, so now many antichrists have come; therefore we know that it is the last hour" (1 Jn. 2, 18).
"We know that we have passed out of death into
life, because we love the brethren. He who does not
love remains in death" (1 Jn. 3, 14). "Whatever is
born of God overcomes the world; and this is the
victory that overcomes the world, our faith" (1 Jn.
5, 4).

At the same time we find the traditional view:
"And now, little children, abide in him, so that when

he appears we may have confidence and not shrink from him in shame at his coming" (1 Jn. 2, 28). "Beloved, we are God's children now; it does not yet appear what we shall be, but we know that when he appears we shall be like him, for we shall see him as he is" (1 Jn. 3, 2). A Christian is actually in communion with God, he is born of God, he possesses God and abides in him.

11

PRECURSORY SIGNS OF
CHRIST'S RETURN

1. The great distress

According to Jewish eschatology the messianic time would be preceded by a period of great distress. The Old Testament speaks about difficulties which would befall the people of God at the end of time. We see e.g. in Ezek. 39 the attack of Gog upon Israel. Daniel speaks about a time of distress: "At that time shall arise Michael, the great prince who has charge of your people. And there shall be a time of trouble, such as never has been since there was a nation till that time" (Dan. 12, 1). "That time" here means the end of time. In this way in rabbinical theology a doctrine was developed about the "labors of the Messiah," an expression which indicated the distress of those days, because this would precede the joys of the coming of the Messiah and of the messianic time. This distress is a time of terror, of turmoil in nature and of uprooting of the moral order.

In the New Testament we find this expectation returning. Here too a time of distress is expected,

previous to the return of Christ. When Christ says
that the false messiahs and prophets, wars and
rumors of war are only "the beginning of the
sufferings" (Mt. 24, 8; Mk. 13, 8), this alludes to the
"labors of the Messiah." Of this time of distress,
which is described in the same manner as the labors
of the Messiah, Christ says: "For then there will be
great tribulation, such as has not been from the beginning of the world until now, no, and never will
be" (Mt. 24, 21; Mk. 13, 19). In this time of distress,
according to the synoptic gospels, the downfall of
Jerusalem and of the Jewish state will occur.

Just as the Jewish eschatology distinguishes between the preceding distress and the messianic times,
so also the synoptic gospels make a distinction between the distress and the return of Christ. Having
described this time of distress Matthew says: "Immediately after the tribulation of those days (24, 29),
and only then follows the description of the return.
Mark does the same: "But in those days, after the
tribulation" (13, 24). Luke places between the two
periods "the time of the nations" (21, 24).

2. The apostasy

The Jewish eschatology expected that in this time
of distress a great apostasy would occur. This expression finds its origin in the remembrance of the
endeavors of king Antioch IV Epiphanes to persuade
the Jews to forsake the religion of Yahweh and to
adopt hellenistic culture.

The New Testament speaks about a great apostasy

which will precede the return of Christ: in the eschatological speech Christ warns against false messiahs and false prophets who would mislead, if this were possible, even the elect (Mt. 24, 23-26; Mk. 13, 21-23). Paul speaks about "the apostasy" which will precede the day of the Lord (2 Thess. 2, 3). Revelation describes how the whole world adored the dragon (the devil) and the beast (the antichrist, Rev. 13, 3-4). As is obvious from the text, this is meant to indicate an apostasy from God, not a political apostasy.

3. The Antichrist

In his second letter to the Thessalonians Paul warns the faithful: "Now concerning the coming of our Lord Jesus Christ and our assembling to meet him we beg you, brethren, not to be quickly shaken in mind or excited, either by spirit or by word, or by letter purporting to be from us, to the effect that the day of the Lord has come. Let no one deceive you in any way; for that day will not come, unless the rebellion comes first, and the man of lawlessness is revealed, the son of perdition, who opposes and exalts himself against every so-called god or object of worship, so that he takes his seat in the temple of God, proclaiming himself to be God. Do you not remember that when I was still with you I told you that? And you know what is restraining him now so that he may be revealed in his time. For the mystery of lawlessness is already at work; only he who now restrains it will do so until he is out of the way. And then the lawless one will be revealed, and the Lord Jesus will slay him with the breath of his mouth and destroy him by his appearing and his coming. The coming of the lawless one by the activity of Satan will be with all power and with pretended signs and wonders, and with all wicked deception of those who are to perish, because they refused to love the truth and so be saved. Therefore God sends upon them a strong delusion, to make them believe what is false, so that all may be condemned who did not believe the truth but had pleasure in unrighteousness" (2 Thess. 2, 1-12).

Paul warns the Thessalonians against some people who assert that the return and the end of the world are not only near, but even standing before the door. These people based their assertion on an inspiration of the Holy Spirit or on Paul himself: as if he would have said or written this. He protests against such an overwrought expectation; the end of the world cannot be near, because a few things must still happen before it. First, a great apostasy must take place; many will allow themselves to be misled by false teachers; moreover the "man of lawlessness" must make his appearance. Paul calls this same personality "the son of perdition," because he will be destroyed by Christ, and be opposed to every so-called god or object of worship. This "man of lawlessness about whom Paul speaks, is usually called "the antichrist." Even though Paul does not use this term, he describes him as the satanic adversary of Christ, as a real counter — christ.

Even though he has not the name, he certainly has the characteristics of an antichrist: Satan works through him as God works through Christ; he has his parousia (coming), as Christ has; he performs miracles as Christ does; he has his followers and leads people to damnation, the same as Christ leads them to salvation. The name "antichrist" which we use is taken from the letters of John; only there is it occasionally used. "Children, it is the last hour; and as you have heard that antichrist is coming, so now many antichrists have come; therefore we know that it is the last hour" (1 Jn. 2, 18). "This is the antichrist, he who denies the Father and the Son" (1 Jn. 2, 22). "Every spirit which does not confess Jesus is not of God. This is the spirit of the antichrist, of which you heard that it was coming, and now it is in the world already" (1 Jn. 4, 3). "For many deceivers have gone out into the world, men who will not acknowledge the coming of Jesus Christ in the flesh; such a one is the deceiver and the antichrist" (2 Jn. 7).

From this admonition of Paul we may conclude that he expects the end of the world will be preceded by the appearance of a power which is inimical to God. There is nothing new in this. In the Old Testament we find the expectation that at the end of time there will be an attack of a power which is inimical to God, which threatens the people of God, but which will be destroyed by God. Ezek. 38-39, a forerunner of these apocalypses, describes the appearance of Gog, the enemy of God, from Magog.

At the end Gog will attack Israel, but God will defeat him. In Revelation we see that at the end of time Satan will have Gog and Magog as his allies in the final combat, and how they are defeated by God (Rev. 20, 7-10). In Daniel the great persecution of Antioch IV Epiphanes is interpreted the same way. The time of persecution is seen as the time of the end, and Antioch is the one who fights against God and the people of God, but he will be destroyed by God. This first great persecution which the Jews underwent made such an impression that Antioch became the traditional representative of the hostile powers at the end of time.

In the New Testament we find this same expectation, e.g. in the text which we quoted from Paul; this too occurs in the synoptics and in Revelation. It is very useful to compare these texts and to notice their great affinity.

In the synoptics we saw that Christ in his eschatological speech announced that his return would be preceded by an appearance of false christs and false prophets and that many would be misled by them (Mt. 24, 3-8; Mk. 13, 5-8; cf. p. 31), and also that the disciples would be persecuted (Mt. 24, 9-13; Mk. 13, 9-13), which is called "the great distress."

The first sign by which this time of the great distress can be recognized according to Matthew and Mark is the "desolating sacrilege." This expression is taken from Daniel, as Matthew himself mentions. There we read the prophecy of the seventy year weeks: "And after the sixty-two weeks, an anointed one shall be cut off, and shall have nothing; and the people of the prince who is to come shall destroy the city and the sanctuary. Its end shall come with a flood, and to the end there shall be war; desolations are decreed. And he shall make a strong covenant with many for one week; and for half of the week he shall cause sacrifice and offering to cease; and upon the wing of abominations shall come one who makes desolate, until the decreed end is poured out on the desolator" (Dan. 9, 26-27).

This passage describes the persecution of Antioch IV; the anointed is the high priest Onias III, who was killed in 171 B.C. the middle of the week of seven years is the year 167, in which the great persecution begins. The "wing of abominations" is probably a pagan emblem which Antiochus had placed in the temple.

Matthew says: "So when you see the desolating sacrilege spoken of by the prophet Daniel, standing in the holy place" (24, 15). Mark says: "But when you see the desolating sacrilege set up where it ought not to be" (13, 14). He indicates the same as Matthew does; moreover he seems to see this desolating sacrilege as a person. It (or he) "destroys" i.e. desolates the holy place, (the temple) by its presence. We therefore must conclude that Jesus is not alluding here to the destruction of Jerusalem, but to a profanation of the temple, one of the events of the great distress, which well precede the return of Christ. This especially, because the persecution of

Antioch, to which allusion is made, is a type of the final combat and of the inimical power which will assert itself at the end of time and will persecute the disciples. Jesus announces here the fulfillment of the prophecy of Daniel. Fleeing, as Jesus exhorts us to do, means fleeing from the enemy of God; this warning still holds good.

We notice that Luke gives a different version of Christ's words: "But when you see Jerusalem surrounded by armies, then know that its desolation has come near. Then let those who are in Judea flee to the mountains" etc. (21, 20-21). He mentions a concrete historical fact, instead of the "desolating sacrilege." From this we may not conclude however that Matthew and Mark mean to indicate the same thing as Luke, viz. the destruction of Jerusalem in 70 A.D., and fleeing from the Romans. Luke's warning regards something from the past and does not hold for all time, as it does in Matthew and Mark.

As has been said, Paul too expects the return of Christ to be preceded by the appearance of a power hostile to God. This enemy, whom we represent as a person, is described in images taken from Daniel's description of Antioch IV: "And the king shall do according to his will; he shall exalt himself and magnify himself above every god" (Dan. 11, 36; cf.: "who opposes and exalts himself against every so-called god or subject of worship" in 2 Thess. 2, 4) and from Ezekiel's mocking song against the king of Tyrus: "Because your heart is proud, and you have said: I am a god, I sit in the seat of the gods, in the heart of the sea, yet you are but a man, and no god, though you consider yourself as wise as a god" (Ezek. 28, 2).

It is very remarkable that Paul, like Matthew and Mark sees a resemblance between the lawless one and Antioch, and that here too the lawless one desecrates the temple, just as the desolating sacrilege did. Considering the close relationship between the synoptic gospels and the two letters to the Thessalonians, it is quite probable that Matthew, Mark and Paul here reflect the same tradition and that they have in mind the same event, viz., the profanation of the temple, which in this case was considered as one of the preceding signs of the end. The desolating sacrilege of Matthew and Mark is the man of lawlessness of Paul therefore, the antichrist.

It is useful to look also to Revelation. In the thirteenth chapter we read: "And I saw a beast rising out of the sea, with ten horns and seven heads, with ten diadems upon its horns and a blasphemous name upon its heads. And the beast that I saw was like a leopard, its feet were like a bear's, and its mouth was like a lion's mouth. And to it the dragon gave his power and his throne and great authority. One of its heads seemed to have a mortal wound, but its mortal wound was healed, and the whole earth followed the beast with wonder. Men worshiped the dragon, for he had given his authority to the beast, and they worshiped the beast, saying: Who is the beast, and who can fight against it? And the beast was given a mouth uttering haughty and blasphemous words, and it was allowed to exercise authority for forty-two months; it opened its mouth to utter blasphemies against God, blaspheming his name and his dwelling, that is, those who dwell in heaven. Also it was allowed to make war on the saints and to conquer them. And authority was given it over every tribe and people and tongue and nation and all who dwell on earth will worship it, every one whose name has not been written before the foundation of the world in the book of life of the Lamb that was slain."

From this description it is evident that the beast is hostile to God: the blasphemous names on the heads (vs. 1), the blasphemies it utters (vs. 6), the fight against the saints (vs. 7). Here too we notice an echo of Daniel. The beast is described in symbols which characterized Antioch IV in Daniel: the mouth full of boasts (vs. 5) "and behold, in this horn . . . a mouth speaking great things" (Dan. 7, 8); the fight against the saints (vs. 7; "as I looked, this horn made war with the saints and prevailed over them": Dan. 7, 21; cf. vs. 25); the forty-two months of the persecution of Antioch, viz. three and a half years; "for a time, two times, and half a time" (Dan. 7, 25), the half year week in Dan. 9, 27. The resemblance of the beast to a lion, a bear, and a leopard (vs. 2) is a composite of the three first beasts of Dan. 7. According to Revelation this beast has the same role as the desolating sacrilege and the man of lawlessness; it curses God's house and demands adora-

tion like God. We can say that in these cases one
and the same personality is meant: the antichrist.

The antichrist according to Revelation 13 was in-
carnate in the Roman empire and especially in one
of the emperors (cf. Rev. 13, 18): "This calls for
wisdom! Let him who has understanding reckon
the number of the beast, for it is a human number,
its number is six hundred and sixty-six." Probably
this is an allusion to Nero. Rome was persecuting
the Christians at that time and John interprets this
as a sign of the end, although he did not want to
say that the end would come later; after this persecution there would still come a time of rest for the
Church, before the end.

This interpretation of John is not proof that the
ancient Christian tradition, found in Matthew, Mark
and Paul, considered Rome the antichrist. For them
the antichrist was connected with the temple. Perhaps they thought some person or other of those
days was the antichrist, but we cannot distinguish
whom they considered such.

In the second letter to the Thessalonians we notice,
however, that Paul remarks that the power of evil
is already active, but that the antichrist for the
moment is still held in check. The Thessalonians
know who or what this obstacle was that kept him
back, but we do not. Judging from what is said
in the eschatological speech: "And this gospel of the
kingdom will be preached throughout the whole
world, as a testimony to all nations; and then the

end will come" (Mt. 24, 14; cf. Mk. 13, 10), one can surmise that Paul was thinking about the preaching of the gospel.

In the above quoted passage (p. 109) from the first and the second letter of John we see that he thinks that the antichrist, or even several antichrists, were already at work in his day. These are persons who preach false doctrines. The presence of such antichrists is for him a sign that the end of time was near. In the same way that he described the return of Christ, the judgment and the eternal life as being already present, he also here describes the antichrist as present.

Scholars have tried hard to determine more exactly the person of the antichrist, but their opinions are widely divergent. The apocalyptic style of the texts makes it very difficult. Nearly all the fathers of the Church and most scholars, Catholics and many non-catholics, consider the antichrist to be an individual person, who at the end of time will persecute the Church. Others consider him to be a symbol of all the enemies of the Church. In the days of the fathers of the Church this enemy was considered to be the Roman empire, later the holy Roman empire; but both these empires have vanished.

The antichrist himself, throughout the centuries, has been given several new names, but he has not kept them. Some saw him incorporated in Mohammed, Luther, Napoleon, etc. The adversaries of the Church, such as the Waldensians, Wyclif, Huss and especially the Reformers called the pope of Rome the antichrist. All these different opinions give evidence of the difficulty in forming an idea about this figure. More important than these guesses about the figure and the time of the antichrist is the text of Paul: "The coming of the lawless one by the activity of Satin will be with all power and with pretended signs and wonders, and with all wicked deception for those who are to perish, because they refused to love the truth and so be saved" (2 Thess. 2, 9-10). This is an echo of Christ's warning: "For false christs and false prophets will arise and show great signs and wonders, so as to lead astray, if possible, even the elect. Lo, I have told you before-hand" (Mt. 24, 24-25; Mk. 13, 22-23).

The power of Satan is still in existence and the Church continuously is exposed to the attacks of her enemies. This is no reason for us to doubt Christ. Only through a firm faith in God and the unshaken conviction that one day "the seats will be placed" for the final judgment (Dan. 7, 9-11) can we hold out in this battle. "Here is a call for the enduration and faith of the saints" (Rev. 13, 10).[8]

12

THE SIGNIFICANCE OF
CHRIST'S RETURN

It is not the intention of the Bible to satisfy our curiosity; it speaks to teach religious truths. This is also true in regard to the return of Christ. It does not teach us anything about the moment at which or the circumstances in which this return will take place, because these things are of no consequence for our eternal happiness. When it speaks of the return, it does so because of the value which this event has for our Christian life.

It is evident that the Bible, in speaking about the return of Christ, often stresses the point that all people will be judged according to their works. This is of great importance for us: our own actions decide our eternal destiny. God is not an indifferent observer. He presents himself as intimately concerned with what we do and will judge us according to what we have done.

In the Old Testament we see how God revealed himself, made known his will and how he will judge people according to the reaction which they have given to this revelation. In the New Testament it is Christ who revealed God to us; we will be judged according to the way we have accepted or rejected this testimony of Christ. "He who receives his testimony sets his seal to this, that God is true. For he whom God has sent utters the words of God, for it is not by measure that he gives the Spirit; the Father loves the Son, and has given all things into his hand. He who believes in the Son has eternal life; he who does not obey the Son shall not see life, but the wrath of God rests upon him" (Jn. 3, 33-36).

The only important thing therefore for us is to accept the word of Christ and to be ready to meet him. Hence all those urgent warnings in the New Testament to be ready: "So then let us not sleep, as others do, but let us keep awake and be sober" (1 Thess. 5, 6). "And it is my prayer that your love may abound more and more, with knowledge and all discernment, so that you may approve what is excellent, and may be pure and blameless for the day of Christ" (Phil. 1, 9-10; cf. pp. 84-85). The return of Christ is the only moment to which the life of a Christian must be orientated. The thought that Christ comes back to judge may frighten us, and this the more so when we pay attention to the descriptions which the synoptics give of this return and when we read: "then all the tribes of the earth will mourn" (Matt. 24, 30), or when we hear about the wrath or the day of wrath (Rom. 2, 5; 1 Thess. 1, 10).

In sermons, the last judgment is often described

as a frightening event. Moreover, every Christian is aware that he is a sinner and that consequently it is possible that he will not persevere.

However, this frightfulness is only one aspect of the return, because Christ does not only come as a judge, but also as a Redeemer: "but our commonwealth is in heaven, and from it we await a Savior, the Lord Jesus Christ" (Phil. 3, 20). "So Christ, having been offered once to bear the sins of many, will appear a second time, not to deal with sin but to save those who are eagerly waiting for him" (Heb. 9, 28). The judgment means punishment for sinners, but reward for the just. In the descriptions of the judgment we can see that the elect are separated from the sinners. Christ has taught us how we can escape the severity of this judgment: "For God has sent the Son into the world, not to condemn the world, but that the world might be saved through him. He who believes in him is not condemned; he who does not believe is condemned already, because he has not believed in the name of the only Son of God" (Jn. 3, 17-18). Christ redeems the faithful from the wrath to come, Paul says (1 Thess. 1, 10). Therefore we too can look forward to the coming of Christ, and a follower of Christ has more reason to look forward to it than to fear it.

It is evident from many passages of the New Testament that the return of Christ is much more an object of desire than of fear. Thus we read at the end of Revelation: "The Spirit and the Bride say: Come!" (22, 17); "Amen! Come, Lord Jesus" (22, 20). In these words we feel the fervent desire of the Christian for the coming of his Lord, but also the desire of his spouse, the Church. The ancient Christians used to pray "Maranatha" (1 Cor. 16, 22), which means: "Our Lord, come!" In the Our Father they prayed: "Thy Kingdom come" (Mt. 6, 10).

Peter encourages the Christians who are persecuted: "Beloved, do not be surprised at the fiery ordeal which comes upon you to prove you, as though something strange were happening to you. But rejoice insofar as you share Christ's sufferings, that you may also rejoice and be glad when his glory is revealed" (1 Pet. 4, 12-13).

James consoles the faithful in their difficulties: "Be patient, therefore, brethren, until the coming of the Lord. Behold, the farmer waits for the precious fruit of the earth, patient over it until it receives the early and the late rain. You also be patient. Establish your hearts, for the coming of the Lord is at hand" (Jas. 5, 7-8).

As we have said before, Paul often refers to the return, when he exhorts his faithful and admonishes them; not in order to frighten them but to point out to them that if they want to enjoy the happiness of the return, they must shape their lives accordingly (cf. pp. 36-38).

For the faithful the return is rather a joyful than of a frightening event. This is evident from the technical term which in the New Testament very often indicates this return, a term which we have taken over in our language: the "parousia."

The Greek word "parousia" was used in hellenistic times to indicate the visit of a king or of some high officer. It is what in Burgundian times was called the "blijde incomste" (the happy entrance): the first visit of a king to a city. On such occasions privileges were given. Such a parousia in antiquity was a great feast. Special taxes were levied to defray the expenses; memorial medals were struck; special religious services were held for the well being of the king. Dressed in white clothes and with wreaths on their heads people went to meet the king in a solemn cortege.

From this use of parousia it is evident therefore that the Christians, at least Paul in his letter, look at the coming of Christ as a glorious event, a coming in magnificence, because the word connotes such splendor.

The description which Paul gives in 1 Thess. 4, 14-18 (cf. pp. 42-44) about the return shows clearly that he takes as his model the civil parousia: the faithful, riding on the clouds, go to meet Christ in the sky. We are reminded also of this by what he says in the same letter: "For what is our hope or joy or crown of boasting before our Lord Jesus at his coming? Is it not you? For you are our glory and joy" (1 Thess. 2, 19-20).

The return of Christ implies the redemption of man in his complete human existence.

By his faith and baptism the Christian has already been redeemed, but as yet only in principle; his redemption is not yet completed; he continues living in this unredeemed world, threatened by the power of evil and subject to the perishable: "We know that the whole creation has been groaning in travail together until now; and not only the creation, but we ourselves, who have the first fruits of the Spirit, groan inwardly as we wait for adoption as sons, the redemption of our bodies. For in this hope we were saved" (Rom. 8, 22-24).

The term "redemption of the body," for Paul, means that our body will be liberated from its decay and from death, to which it was subject in its unredeemed condition. A Christian looks forward with great desire to the moment when his body will be liberated from the burden, and this will happen at the resurrection and the glorification. Then the fulfillment will be a fact, and with body and soul the Christian will share the glorified life of Christ: "When Christ who is our life appears, then you also will appear with him in glory" (Col. 3, 4).

It is a fact that at his death man is liberated from the power of evil and that his soul receives its reward, because since the death of Christ the souls of the faithful departed, which are purified of all stains, will be admitted even before the return of Christ and before the resurrection of their bodies to the beatific vision, as Pope Benedict pronounced in 1336. Consequently, since that time, especially in the West, more and more attention was given to the happiness of the soul. This is certainly a true aspect of eschatology; the Bible speaks about the happiness to be enjoyed immediately after death. Christ said to the good thief: "Truly, I say to you, today you will be with me in Paradise" (Lk. 23, 43). Paul knows that after his death he will be united with Christ: "We are of good courage, and we would rather be away from the body and at home with the Lord" (2 Cor. 5, 8). "I am hard pressed between the two. My desire is to depart and be with Christ, for that is far better" (Phil. 1, 23). Still these are only a few sporadic passages: usually the attention of the authors of the New Testament, and of Paul, is drawn toward the return of Christ; this is more exact.

We know that after death the **soul** is beatified, but the **man** is beatified only at the general resurrection; the complete redemption of man therefore commences only at the end of time, at the return of Christ. It is a pity that we usually fail to pay attention to this, and that the resurrection of the body in which we believe is often considered as something extra which we receive in addition to the beatitude of the soul. In our day, now that the body is more appreciated, the glorification of man — body and soul — should receive more attention.

From this it follows that the return of Christ is the final fulfillment of God's plan of redemption.

This glorification of the elect is the last event in the plan of salvation.

The return of Christ constitutes the final victory of God and of Christ. God's plan is completed.

Then takes place the final reckoning with sin, the only enemy of God: "And the devil, who had deceived them was thrown into the lake of fire and brimstone where the beast and the false prophet were, and they will be tormented day and night for ever and ever" (Rev. 20, 10). "For he (Christ) must reign until he has put all his enemies under his feet" (1 Cor. 15, 25). This is the moment when God's royal sovereignty achieves its full reality: "When all things are subjected to him, then the Son himself will also be subjected to him who put all things under him, that God may be everything to every one" (1 Cor. 15, 28). After sin and death have been destroyed, God will permeate his elect with his light and his beatitude.

We see that the authors of the New Testament, in speaking about the return, always regarded the realization of God's plan and the glory of God.

This victory of God and of Christ must be for us the overpowering motive to look forward with desire to the return of Christ; and Christ himself taught us to pray for this: "Hallowed be thy name. Thy kingdom come, Thy will be done, on earth as it is in heaven" (Mt. 6, 9-10).

REFERENCES

1. P. Schoonenberg, S.J.: *Het geloof van ons doopsel.* III ('s Hertogenbosch 1958) p. 225.

2. W. Grossouw: "De hoop der christenen volgens Sint-Paulus," *Ned. Kath. Stemmen* 51 (1955) p. 271.

3. G. Thils: "Espérance et sens chrétien de l'histoire," *Lumen Vitae* 9 (1954) p. 497.

4. P. Schoonenberg S.J.: "Arbeid - Verlossing - Eindvolharding." *Verbum* 27 (1957) p. 296.

5. P. Schoonenberg S.J.: "Zo zullen we altijd bij de Heer zijn." *Verbum* 24 (1957) p. 296.

6. F. X. Durwell: *La resurrection de Jesus, mystere de salut.* (Le Puy, Paris 1950) pp. 275-276.

7. C. H. Dodd: *The Interpretation of the fourth Gospel.* (Cambridge 1958) p. 395.

8. J. Nelis s.s.s.: "Daniel" *(De Boeken van het Oude Testament* XI, 2 Roermond, Maaseik 1954) p. 21.